hi everybody,
I hope you Love our book and it makes You happy
we work very hard.
I am GENERATION G!!!
I will Fight For you
will You Fight For me?

I Love you
Peace OUT
Love
GiGi ♡♡♡
PS I hope you Love our Picture.

MOM wrote This For me
I hope You Love My Book
I Love Fox VALLY ever

Love gigi ♡♡♡

#GenerationG

A True Story of Miracles, Hope, and
Unconditional Acceptance

NANCY GIANNI

#GENERATION G
A TRUE STORY OF MIRACLES, HOPE, AND UNCONDITIONAL ACCEPTANCE

iUniverse books may be ordered through booksellers or by contacting:

iUniverse
1663 Liberty Drive
Bloomington, IN 47403
www.iuniverse.com
1-800-Authors (1-800-288-4677)

ISBN: 978-1-5320-4221-8 (sc)
ISBN: 978-1-5320-4223-2 (hc)
ISBN: 978-1-5320-4222-5 (e)

Library of Congress Control Number: 2018902629

Print information available on the last page.

iUniverse rev. date: 03/13/2018

This book is first dedicated to my kids, Franco, Romi, Bella, and GiGi, and my husband, Paul. Your continued support of my relentless pursuit to make this world a better place has made us all the crazy, awesome, fun, committed family we are today.

For **EVERY** GiGi's Playhouse founder, president, VP, treasurer, site coordinator, family, donor, tutor, volunteer, toilet cleaner, floor washer, advocate, and intern and all the rest of you who helped build GiGi's Playhouse and make it all it is today. I truly thank you from the bottom of my heart. You are all warriors who continue to change the world with all you have done.

For my amazing friends! You know who you are and understand my motto of "work hard and play hard!" Thank you for doing both with me to help make all this happen. 99!

To my little angels in heaven—though you can no longer come to our playhouse, I feel your love from heaven. I pray for your guidance every day. Your voices will never be forgotten.

To my angels on earth who believe in my model of giving everything away for free for the greater good.

And most importantly to GiGi, for teaching me to be better every day and to never give up!

In loving memory of my mom, June Stinger.
Through her selfless hard work,
she showed me that belief and love can change the world.

Contents

Introduction

I sat quietly at the awards dinner, hanging on every word. I listened to the emcee introducing the winner, awed by this woman's accomplishments. She was described as an entrepreneur, an innovator, and a selfless warrior. She was called a mother, a leader, and a believer. *I want to meet this woman!* I thought.

Then they called my name. I looked up, and the emcee was motioning for me to join him on the stage. I felt my stomach flip, and I became instantly nauseated. On shaky legs, I stood up slowly, placing my napkin on the table and holding on to the back of my chair. *They can't possibly be talking about me,* I thought. *I can't fill those shoes. What about wine-drinking, country music–loving, party-going Nancy? Can I be that Nancy too?*

I looked around at all the people standing and clapping for me, and I fought to quell the nervousness rising in my throat. Still shaky, I began to walk toward the stage. I wasn't sure how to be that person, the woman they had all come to honor. I felt like I exhibited, at most, two of the qualities the emcee attributed to me—and that would be on my best days. (And I still feel that way.) But I would never describe myself in those terms. It all seemed to be referring to someone else, to someone much more accomplished and important than I could ever claim to be.

Most of what I've accomplished has been through miracles—in many forms and in many places. I didn't make it all happen; I believed in the potential of what I could make happen, and then I worked my tail off to make the most of the countless gifts that manifested. Miracles, one and all. Yes, I'm a big believer in miracles. But over time, I've learned that miracles are not always pretty or obvious; sometimes you have to search for them. Miracles may even be disguised in pain or tragedy. But it's what you do with the pain that brings the miracle to light. Finding that inner strength to harness the good in a situation propels you to action. Lots of us think we don't have that capacity. We look at others struggling with illness and discrimination and loss, and we think, *I could never do that* or *I'm not strong enough to get through that.* But I'm here to tell you that you *can* and you *are!* Don't think you don't have that strength. You are born with it. We all have it; sometimes we just have to find it.

I'm living proof of that. Fifteen years ago, I didn't know that the birth of my daughter GiGi and the shock of her Down syndrome diagnosis would be a miracle, but let me tell you—it has triggered a series of miracles that are changing the world every single day. I just had to know where to look and to pull the positive from the situation.

Inwardly, I reminded myself of all this as I took the stage at the awards dinner. The applause died down as the crowd waited for me to speak, and I took a deep breath and thought of GiGi, my beautiful daughter—now a teenager! When did *that* happen? She's the catalyst behind all of this. I do what I do for GiGi—I'm a mom first and foremost—but she is by no means the *only* reason I do what I do. I have this vision of a world—not that far away—that is accepting of everyone. All our differences, all our "otherness," and all our unique abilities will be accepted and encouraged. That's what we're really working toward. We call it Generation G because it's about global acceptance for all. (As you read this book, you'll learn more about our plan of action to bring about this global acceptance.) We may have started with Down syndrome because it's close to our family and our hearts, but the ultimate goal is much bigger. And we need people to join us.

I think that people, by nature, want to do good things. It's part of what makes us human. But often, there are too many outside distractions that take the place of decency, human kindness, and even human contact! We have a tendency to think that it's others who need the help—not us or someone we know. But the truth is that all of us are one step away from being different or loving someone who is different. It could happen with a simple fall off a bike, the birth of a new baby or grandbaby, or a debilitating illness. Differences do not discriminate. They don't care who you are. They don't care that you're "low risk" or "not one of *those* kind of people." Being different is the ultimate leveler, and it could happen to you in mere seconds from now. When you experience that difference in yourself or someone you love, things change drastically, and you'll find yourself yearning for a more accepting world. But why wait until that happens? Let's start now.

It's a lot of work, of course. It's exhausting, often heartrending and gut-wrenching, and frequently frustrating. I long for help, a break, or someone else to pick up the reins for a while so I can take a deep breath and relax for a moment. I dream about the day when I can live in that moment of the accomplishment and not worry about the next thing that needs to be done. But then I always realize that GiGi doesn't get to take a break from her diagnosis; no one does. People who are different don't get to shed that "differentness" at the end of the day. They struggle constantly for acceptance. I think about the promise I made to GiGi: that I would work to achieve acceptance of those with Down syndrome and, ultimately, acceptance for all. We've made great strides, particularly as we launch Generation G, but we're not there yet.

Looking at the empty glass of wine in front of my place at the table, knowing it will be full as soon as my speech is over, I let out the breath I didn't realize I'd been holding. And then I looked over at GiGi and my other kids. They've given me the courage to speak, to let these people in on the miracles of my life and our greater mission. I might not feel like the superhero the emcee made me out to be—and I'm still not sure I deserve the award they are bestowing on me—but I do know that with enough heart, passion, and, yes, miracles, we can inspire others to take up the cause of worldwide acceptance for all.

And if we do that—if even one person hears my message and is driven to take action—it will all have been worth it.

I believed that as I accepted my award that night, and I believe it now. And so, I will launch your reading this book with the same words I used to begin my acceptance speech: "Thank you. I'm Nancy Gianni. I'm GiGi's mom."

Who am I to have total control of this tiny little life,
and what have I done to deserve this?

CHAPTER 1

The Power—and Miracle— of Becoming a Mom

In case I haven't made it completely clear before now, my most important role in life is that of Mom. Being a mom is an awesome responsibility and incredible gift. It's a miracle, plain simple. It's also what means the most to me and what brings me the most joy. Before I share the story of Generation G and GiGi's Playhouse, I first have to share my experience of motherhood–becoming Mom to GiGi, my youngest child, and to her three older siblings before that. If you don't understand my journey, why should you trust me as a source of wisdom or support on your own journey? My style is to tell it like it is, and that's exactly what I'm going to do throughout this book. Here's our story.

Twenty one years ago, I learned that I had been given both great power and great responsibility. I felt like a superhero. It was twenty one years ago that my eldest child, Franco, was born. Like any first-time mother, I was happy beyond belief, overwhelmed, head over heels in love, and scared that someone had given me this baby and I had no idea what I was doing. I realized that it didn't matter how many books I'd read or how many nieces or nephews I'd babysat over the years; until you're sitting alone in the nursery with your crying baby in your arms, you can't possibly know what to do.

One evening, when Franco was brand-new and still pink, he was crying and crying, and nothing we tried to calm him down was working. My husband, Paul, paced back and forth in the nursery, his face screwed up into a mask of concern. He was worried. Franco looked for all the world like he was in terrible distress, and Paul was trying to help me. Nothing was working.

Franco's birth had been difficult. I'd been put on Pitocin to induce labor because it wasn't happening naturally. Despite the drugs and the best efforts of the doctors and nurses at the hospital, labor still didn't happen. They sent me home, telling me we'd try again in a day or two. On the way out of the hospital, I felt like a failure, like my body couldn't do the one thing it had been designed to do. I felt inadequate.

That evening, when we got home, all I wanted was to meet this child; I didn't want to wait until he was ready. I was impatient! I walked the entire length of the golf course on the edge of our property—back and forth—to try to bring on labor. I have never been the sort of person to leave things up to chance, so I did the only thing I could think of to try to hurry my baby along: I walked. I went into labor the following morning.

Even though labor had started, my body was still being stubborn. I spent the morning pacing the halls of the hospital—just as I'd done on the golf course the night before—trying to get my water to break. It felt like every part of my body—save my mind—was telling me it wasn't ready for this. Clearly, my body was refusing to let go until it was absolutely ready. I didn't know what else to do; I kept walking.

Finally, the doctor came in and broke my water. We talked, chatting about who knows what, until the nurse looked at the monitor and her expression changed. She tapped the monitor.

"Hmm," she said. "The monitor must not be working. We lost the baby's heartbeat."

Those are among the most terrifying words a mother-to-be in labor can hear. The doctor, realizing what would happen, called a Code Red. The nurse had rehooked me up to all the monitors, and, suddenly, the fetal heart-rate monitor began to beep. When the doctor broke my water, the baby had slid down, and the umbilical cord had gotten stuck between my cervix and the baby's shoulder. He was wedged in, and his heart rate continued to drop.

Instantly, the room was full of doctors, nurses, and specialists. Through the crowd, I saw Paul, standing in the corner, looking more scared than I'd ever seen him. I wanted to tell him that I'd be okay, that the baby would be okay, but I didn't know that. I couldn't reassure him.

"We need to turn you over," the doctor said to me. "We need to try to get the baby loose."

As you can imagine, a woman nine months pregnant and ready to deliver, attached to numerous machines and tubes, isn't the easiest creature to maneuver. The doctors and nurses tried for a moment to jostle Franco loose, but he was stuck fast.

"We have to get her into OR, *stat*," I heard a nurse say.

The doctor looked at the fetal heart-rate monitor and then back at me. "There's no time," he said. "We have to take the baby now."

I looked back, as my bed was wheeled down the hall, and saw Paul, worry creasing his brow. No one was telling him anything.

"I'm going in," the doctor said.

I weakly reached out to Paul, who was no longer in the room. "I'm still awake," I said in a feeble voice. "I'm still awake."

At that moment, all I could picture was Fred Flintstone coming into the room, using a club to knock me out. That was what I wanted; I didn't want to be awake for any of this. The anesthesiologist administered the sedative, but I could still see the faces of the doctors and nurses swimming above me. "Wait," I wanted to tell them. "Wait! I'm not ready."

When I woke up, the first thing I saw was Paul, sitting in a chair in the corner of the room, holding Franco. He held him up for me to see. I smiled, and he brought the baby over to me and laid him on my chest.

The doctors and nurses were still buzzing around the room, but they seemed to be moving at half speed, not rushing like they had been before. A nurse checked my vital signs, tested Franco's reflexes, and consulted a chart.

"Seven minutes," the doctor said.

It took me a moment to realize he was talking to me. "Hmm?" I asked. "What's that?" I couldn't stop staring at the tiny baby in my arms.

"Seven minutes," he repeated. "That's how long from the time the IV went in until we got the baby out: seven minutes."

I looked at Paul, confused.

"That's a hospital record," the nurse said, smiling and adjusting the pillows behind my head.

"The baby's fine," the doctor continued. "He scored high on the Apgar. There's no brain damage. We got him out in time."

I looked at Paul again. He still looked worried. I wondered why.

"But," the doctor said and then stopped.

With that one word, I felt my heart drop into my stomach. As a parent, it's the one word you never want to hear at such a time. My heart began beating faster as I waited for the doctor to continue.

"But," he repeated, "we had to cut you to get him out. It ... wasn't pretty."

I looked over at Paul again. He nodded slowly.

"But the baby is fine?" I asked nervously.

The doctor patted me on the shoulder. "The baby is fine; perfectly healthy," he said. "But the incision we made had to be vertical. We had no choice about that; we didn't have time to waste."

"Okay," I said, not really paying attention. Instead, I focused all my energy on the tiny, new, perfectly healthy person in my arms.

"It might make it difficult for you in subsequent pregnancies," the doctor said. "You'll have to be monitored closely to make sure the incision doesn't rupture."

"Mm-hmm," I said, nearly ignoring him completely. At that moment, I didn't care about future pregnancies; I didn't care about incisions; I didn't care about sutures; I didn't even care about my ride down the hallway on all fours. I cared only that my baby, my firstborn, was healthy. I looked down at Franco and thought about how blessed we were. The road to get there hadn't been easy, but the challenge had made it all the more worth it.

A few weeks later, as Paul paced the nursery, with a crying Franco in his arms, unable to calm him, I sat in the rocking chair in the corner of the room and wondered if his birth had been the easy part.

"Here," I said, reaching out to take Franco. "Give him to me."

Paul gently placed Franco in my arms, and I sat with him, rocking back and forth. Franco continued to cry. Quietly, Paul left the room, and I was alone with my son.

I looked down at him, at his tiny little face screwed up and wrinkled from crying. He was red and wailing. I said nothing. Instead, I rocked him and touched his face gently with my hand. I didn't pat him or shush him or beg him to stop crying; I simply placed my hand on his cheek. Almost instantly, his tears slowed, the wailing stopped, and he calmed down. Like magic, I had been able to make my son calm down with only a touch. I looked at my hand, amazed and yet humbled by the power I had. I was struck by a realization: *Here I am, a first-time mom, and this little tiny baby is in my arms crying. Putting my palm to his face instantly calmed him down.* I was overwhelmed with the awe-inspiring amount of power I had. Why was I given that? What had I done to deserve it?

A second wave of emotion hit me right after the first. I was filled with gratitude—gratitude that, as a mother, I had that power to comfort my son, to transfer my love and protection to him with a touch.

And then I felt a sense of responsibility like I had never known before. When I was pregnant, of course, I felt responsible for this little person growing inside me. He was completely dependent on me for everything, and I did my best to make sure that he'd be ready for everything that came his way once he arrived in this world. But, until that moment when I had calmed Franco with just a touch of my hand, I hadn't realized that my responsibility was far greater than I'd ever imagined. I was a mother; I was responsible for raising my child to become who he was going to be. I was responsible for instilling in him confidence, generosity, grace, and independence. That was all up to me. I had never felt such responsibility before. I looked down at my son, now sleeping soundly in my arms, and I realized that by giving birth to this child, I was given a great power and a great responsibility. I was determined not to waste either one.

That moment made me take being a mom very seriously. I had always known that I wanted children—multiple children—and I had always assumed that I'd have them. I had Franco when I was thirty and thought I'd have a few more children in subsequent years. Compared to Franco's birth, I imagined the others would be easy. What I never anticipated was just how difficult becoming a mother again would be.

Two years later, Paul and I remained unsuccessful in having another child. We began investigating in fertility treatments and other options after our best efforts yielded no success. Specialists told us that his sperm and my eggs were not compatible. What *the–*? I had Franco with no problem, and now his little swimmers have turned on me? How could that be?

Anyone who has been through IVF (in vitro fertilization) or artificial insemination, and all the hormones and drugs that come with them, will tell you that pretty soon, you start feeling more like a lab experiment than a human. Doctors naturally want to perform the procedure that has the highest probability of success, so they begin looking at you as a number instead of a patient. Combine that with the fact that I spent months being poked, prodded, and monitored while being told to pee on a stick at frequent intervals, and, after two years, I'd had it. While fertility treatments may be clinical to medical professionals, to those of us trying to have a child, they are the most personal thing imaginable. And when they don't work and your body doesn't cooperate, you feel a crushing sense of disappointment and failure. It doesn't matter how often you see that single pink line on the pregnancy test; it's devastating every time.

By the time Franco was three, Paul and I had been through four rounds of IVF and six rounds of artificial insemination, and we had nothing to show for it but fragile psyches and broken hearts. I had become so accustomed to the nurse's voice on the phone, calling with another negative pregnancy test result, that I could tell instantly from her voice when the news wasn't good—and it was never good. After a while, I honestly didn't think my heart could take another "Hi, hon," in a consoling tone from a well-meaning nurse. Paul said I wouldn't have to; he promised he'd answer the calls from that point on.

One day, while waiting for the results from my latest test, Paul and I packed Franco into his stroller and took him to the Memorial Day parade downtown. Standing there among the proud veterans and happy people, I could almost forget my own personal struggle and pain. We found a prime spot right alongside the parade route, and we settled in, Franco playing with toys in his stroller and pointing at all the brightly colored red, white, and blue balloons.

"I'm going to get something to eat," Paul said. "I'll be back in a few minutes."

I nodded and reached down to adjust Franco's T-shirt. Paul wandered away, and as I saw him disappear into the crowd, the cell phone in the stroller rang. I looked at the caller ID and saw it was my doctor's office calling. *Damn it, Paul,* I thought. *I'm not supposed to have to answer these calls anymore.* I debated not answering it, just letting it go to voice mail. *After all,* I told myself, *It's never good news. Why should this time be any different?*

But something made me answer the phone. "Hello?" I said, my guard already up, expecting the worst—fully prepared for it—and that prepared, negative part of me was trying to squash that little bit of hope that still burned inside.

"Hi, hon," the nurse said in that all-too-familiar tone.

I didn't let her finish. I knew the drill; I had gotten this call seemingly countless times before. I knew it by heart.

"Right, thanks," I told her. "Got it. Thanks for calling."

She tried to console me, as she always did. She tried to talk about next steps. I didn't let her get a word in. "Gotta go," I said. "Thanks." And I hung up.

I tossed the phone back into the stroller and just stood there, too numb with sadness over another failed attempt, pissed off at my body for not doing what it was genetically programmed to do, and hating the fact that people felt sorry for me. I couldn't stand it when people felt sorry for me. To me, that meant that I was inadequate, worthy of only pity and sympathy. And I didn't want any of it.

I stood there for a few moments in the sunshine, with people cheering and smiling all around me, but I wasn't *really* seeing anything. And then, suddenly, I felt a shift. I felt the earth move. I glanced down at Franco, playing in his stroller, and felt as if my eyes had miraculously been opened.

Look at this beautiful son you have right here, I told myself. *Look at all these brave men and women.* I looked up and down the street, seeing proud veterans everywhere. *These people risked their lives for you and this country, and you're standing here feeling sorry for yourself.* A little boy with a walker passed by, his mother beside him. I watched him go, saw him smile, and realized that, in fact, I had it good. I had a wonderful husband who loved me—even if he did need a hot dog at the worst-possible time—a beautiful, healthy son, and a loving, supportive community. I remembered back to that feeling I'd had when I realized I had the power to calm my crying son. I was grateful; I needed to remember to always be grateful. At that moment, I made the decision that I was done with fertility treatments. I was done feeling like a science experiment and like my hormones were in control of my life. I just wanted to be me again. I tried to tell myself that some things were not under my control and I had to just let them be. It went against every fiber of my being, but I let it go; I stopped trying to control everything.

That winter, I took Franco to the mall to meet Santa and do some

Christmas shopping. While we were there, we passed the food court, where I saw a crowd of kids with special needs.

"Field trip?" I asked the teacher who was overseeing the group.

"They're all here to see Santa Claus," she told me. "They love it."

I smiled and watched the children. Despite their challenges, I realized they were no different than Franco, who tugged on my leg, urging me to take him to Santa. "Is it okay if I buy them some cookies?" I asked the teacher, wanting to do something for this group of children and their teachers.

"I think that would be great," she said, smiling.

A few moments later, as I was handing out the cookies—and giving some to Franco to distribute as well—a little boy with Down syndrome gave me the biggest smile I'd ever seen. His wide-open joyful face nearly floored me. "Hi," I said, crouching down to look him in the eye. "I'm Nancy. What's your name?"

"Joey!" he said, proud.

"It's very nice to meet you, Joey," I told him.

Later that afternoon, after Franco and I had visited Santa and seen Joey and his friends again, we were walking out to the car. I saw a school bus pull up. All of the children from the food court formed a line to get on. Stepping up the bus stairs was Joey. Without a word—how did he even know we were there—he turned around and waved at us, his smile huge. I waved right back. I could not get Joey out of my head. I knew I was meant to meet him that day, but I was not sure why. I have always been drawn to individuals with Down syndrome, and I felt that Joey needed me in some way, even though I couldn't imagine how or why that would be.

That evening, when we got back home, I asked Paul, "What about adoption?" He stared at me, waiting for me to continue. I told him about meeting the children at the mall and about Joey, how he had been drawn to me and how I felt that he needed me. I explained that I instinctively needed to make sure he was okay.

"Nancy," Paul said, trying to reassure me, "I'm sure he's fine. He probably has parents who love him and care about him."

"But what if he doesn't?" I asked. "I have to know that he's okay."

Never being one to let things go, my pledge to cease trying to control things notwithstanding, I called the school-bus company and found out what schools it serviced. Then, I called around and tried to figure out where Joey went to school. Of course, no one could tell me anything. Looking back on it now, I realized how silly and/or crazy I must have sounded on the phone. And as a parent, I am thankful that schools are not in the habit of divulging information about their students to anyone who calls!

The point, though, was largely moot. Exhausted from fertility treatments and the emotional roller coaster we'd been on, Paul had no interest in adopting. He thought it would be too difficult and that we'd be setting ourselves up for even more disappointment. But, finally, with much cajoling on my part—and because he could see how desperately I wanted another child—Paul agreed to explore adoption.

We spoke with an attorney and were put in touch with a woman who was half Irish and half Italian. The match couldn't have been more perfect: I am a full-on proud Irish girl, and Paul is 100 percent Italian! Excited, we met with the birth mother, and, because she'd had drug issues in the past, I asked her to agree to be examined by my doctor to ensure that everything was all right. The woman got angry; she didn't like that I was demanding accountability from her. I started to feel sick to my stomach. *It had seemed so perfect, and yet, we were going to lose another baby.*

The next morning, I was at the gym with my best friend, Denise. I was working out all the anger, hurt, and confusion I felt from the past four years. She and I had bonded and become close because she'd had a baby who died at birth. She'd gone through unimaginable pain, and yet, she was still such a strong support for me.

Again, I started to feel queasy. Thinking it was stress and anxiety, I pushed myself harder.

"Maybe you're pregnant," Denise said, looking me up and down.

"Oh, yeah. Okay," I said, cynically. "There's no way."

"Well," she said as she watched me pound the machine, "maybe you should take a test anyway. What do you have to lose?"

What I couldn't properly articulate to her was that I felt like I had everything to lose—everything. I honestly didn't think I could handle getting another single pink line. And her simple mention of the fact that I might be pregnant had rekindled that desire within me. I couldn't turn it off. I couldn't face another disappointment. I'd started getting rid of Franco's baby things, sad that I wouldn't need them again. I told myself that if I got the baby things out of the house, I could make room for something new in my life. Plus, I would no longer be constantly faced with the reminder that there weren't going to be any more babies in our house. But then I realized that this was coming from a woman who had lost her baby at birth. I took a deep breath and realized that if she had made it through that, I could take the damn test and handle another disappointment. The perspective she provided me was important.

And so, my friend wore me down. "At least you'll know," she said. "And then you can move forward with the adoption."

"Fine," I relented. "If I take the test, will you shut up and then go drink with me?"

She responded like any best friend would. "Hell, yeah!"

That evening, I drove to the train station to pick up Paul. I saw him get off the train and walk toward the car. Unable to help myself, I grabbed the Nordstrom bag off the seat next to me and got out of the car, jogging to meet him.

"Hi," he said, surprised that I'd come to meet him. "What's going on?"

I shoved the bag in his hands. "Look," I said.

Paul, confused, slowly opened the bag and pulled out the pink-and-white stick. "Nancy, what—" he said, looking down at the stick in his hands.

"I'm pregnant," I said.

Paul stared at me in complete disbelief. I had never even shared with him the remote possibility I could be pregnant. Like me, he was afraid to believe it, afraid to let his heart go there, only to be ripped out again.

I started laughing, crying, and screaming.

Finally, he just grabbed me and picked me up.
We did it! We really did it!

Despite how badly I'd wanted a second child and how hard we'd tried for years to have one, I felt instantly guilty when I realized that Franco was going to have to share me with a sibling. To be honest, with only one child for almost four years, I'd become a total freak of a mom. I was the very definition of a helicopter parent. I'd read somewhere that children can choke on the skins of grapes and hot dogs, so I peeled Franco's grapes and removed the skins from his hot dogs for years. I'm telling you, I was nuts. There wasn't a moment when I wasn't hovering over him or tending to his needs, regardless of whether he actually needed anything. Franco was a high-maintenance boy because I had made him that way; it was totally my fault. So, when I realized we were finally going to have a second child, I was afraid of how he'd handle it. Even then, a part of me knew that I was going to ruin this child if something didn't change.

Unfortunately, my second pregnancy wasn't a complete walk in the park. Because of the surgery I'd had when Franco was born, this was considered a high-risk pregnancy, and so I was scheduled for a C-section. As a result of all this, the doctor paid a lot of attention to me and wanted to see me often. One day, Paul and I were in the obstetrician's office for an ultrasound, and the technician thought he detected something on the screen. He stared at it and called in the doctor. They consulted quietly. All the while, I was panicking. The last thing you want to do around a pregnant woman—particularly one who'd tried so hard to get pregnant in the first place—is talk about her ultrasound in hushed tones. There's no way she's *not* going to freak out. I was a mess. I could feel my heart pounding.

The doctor thought he might have seen something in the baby's brain on the ultrasound. He ordered more tests. Of course, I was terrified. He didn't put me through anything too invasive, but when you're pregnant, every possibility is terrifying.

Eventually, the doctor concluded that what he'd seen was probably a shadow on the ultrasound. I couldn't believe it. I kept thinking that if this had happened ten years before, technology wouldn't have progressed to the point where the ultrasound was so strong that it was picking up shadows in my uterus! *How could he see shadows?* I wondered. *It's pretty dark in there! How does he know he saw a shadow?*

The doctor, while wonderful and with the best intentions, made me nervous because of his hovering. I admit I was a helicopter parent with Franco, and he was definitely a helicopter doctor. Eventually, he must have realized that he was panicking me with every visit, and so he tried to calm me.

"Remember that I said it was probably just a shadow," my doctor said on a subsequent visit, attempting to reassure me.

"Probably" wasn't good enough for me if there was something potentially wrong with my baby.

"Maybe it's something that your family just has, but it's probably no big deal," he said.

There was that word again. I tried to calm down, tried to put my faith in the doctor and his staff. But I never did get a clear answer.

Meanwhile, while I was pregnant, we bought a new house. Because I have always been an all-or-nothing type of person, I thought, *What better time to buy a new house, start a new project, and be multitasking like crazy than when I'm eight months pregnant?* But in the end, the move was a blessing for our family and for my relationship with Franco. As I mentioned, this baby's delivery was scheduled. In a way, it was reassuring to know that I was going to show up at the hospital on the appointed day, have the surgery at the scheduled time, and be handed a baby. I wouldn't be the loser who couldn't be coaxed into labor with Pitocin; I would do it right this time.

From our new house, I had enrolled Franco in a new school. My plan was for my children to go to Catholic school, and I was going to drive them instead of having them take the bus. But since the baby— whom we would name Isabella (Bella, for short)—was scheduled to be born on September 12, I knew that for a little while, Franco would have to take the bus until I could drive him again. Because I was hovering and worried about him, I thought it would be too big of an adjustment for him to start the year being driven to school, then have to take the bus once his baby sister was born, and, ultimately, transition back to being driven once I was back in the swing of things. So, I made what was, at the time, the heartbreaking decision to send four year old Franco to school on the bus at the start of the school year. It was hard for me; I felt like I was throwing him to the wolves. I wanted to drive him to school so that he'd have only my influence for a longer time. I was afraid of what he'd be subjected to otherwise. To put this another way, he was my baby, and I wanted to be his major source of influence. I did not want anyone to hurt him, and I certainly did not want him to think it was okay to hurt others or make fun of people just because he saw others doing it. I imagined riding the bus would result in these experiences, whereas my driving him would be a 100 percent nurturing experience. Boy, did I have a lot to learn!

Franco's new school started at 7:00 a.m., which meant the bus picked him up at 6:15. Thinking back to my tiny little pre-kindergartener son ascending the bus steps, having to stretch his tiny legs to make the climb, I can't believe I was able to do it. I followed that bus to school for at least the first week because, like I said, I was a crazy, hovering helicopter mom. But I just couldn't help it.

I realize now, of course, that having Franco take the bus and meet new children and become part of his new school without his crazy pregnant mother holding his hand and hovering over him all the time was one of the best things I could have done for him; it did wonders for his ability to develop a sense of independence, and it helped his socialization skills too. But at the time, it nearly broke my heart.

Part of it was that I was still feeling guilty about how Franco would feel when Bella was born. He'd been the love of my life for nearly four years, and all of a sudden, he'd have to share me with someone else. I'd have to spread out my love. I felt like I was betraying him. But I underestimated Franco. The second Bella was born—on schedule and with no drama, just like I'd wanted—there was nothing but joy. I saw Bella's dimples for the first time, and I thought, *This is how it's supposed to be.* I'd wanted to be present for all of it, and I was.

From day one, Franco loved Bella and would give anything for her. He didn't have a jealous bone in his body. I watched him kiss his new baby sister and wondered how he'd ended up that way—so giving and loving after I'd hovered and nearly spoiled him rotten. I was blissful, and completely grateful for my family.

At the same time, Paul and I were both dealing with family medical issues. Paul's sister Giovanna was fighting cancer. My brother was immersed in an ongoing battle with schizophrenia. We were both very close to our siblings, and throughout my pregnancy and our move, we were caring for both Paul's sister and my brother. Their struggles and diagnoses also served to make us even more grateful for the two healthy, happy children we had. But the cloud of these diagnoses always hung over our heads. Our children couldn't always be in the forefront because we had this tremendous responsibility for our siblings. So, as grateful as we were, we had other concerns.

For almost the first year, I breast-fed Bella. She was much more independent than Franco, which I think tends to happen with second children. Whereas Franco had been more cautious and careful—partially, I'm sure, because I never left him alone for more than ten seconds—Bella was curious, inquisitive, and into everything. Whereas it had been difficult to wean Franco, it was much easier with Bella. Despite our concerns and responsibilities regarding our siblings, life was good, and Paul and I were happy. We traveled a lot and worked out all the time. We were enjoying life. We weren't actively trying to have another child because we both remembered the hell we'd gone through before having Bella. Neither of us wanted to go back to those feelings of disappointment and inadequacy. Plus, didn't his sperm hate me? They must have had a drunken night when they gave us Bella!

When Bella was fourteen months old, Paul and I were out for drinks with one of his biggest clients. I wasn't breast-feeding anymore, so we were all drinking and having fun and acting crazy. From out of the blue, Paul's client started telling offensive, off-color jokes. He was using the *n*-word and the *r*-word, making me cringe. I think he was trying to impress his date, but none of it sat right with me. Normally, I would have just stood up and walked away, or let it go. After all, this man was such an important client that his business allowed us many luxuries. But, that night, something deep inside wouldn't allow me to let it go.

I felt immense anger welling up in me. "What makes you think you can talk like that in front of me?" I asked him. "Why do you think you can talk about people like that?"

Paul tried to hush me, embarrassed that I was calling out one of his biggest clients. But I couldn't let it go. I didn't mean to sound as harsh as I did, but I couldn't help it; I laid into the guy.

The client tried to backpedal, talking about his experiences with groups of people that weren't positive. But he was clearly embarrassed.

Paul was mortified, and on our way to dinner at a restaurant, he really let me have it. "What the hell, Nancy?" he said. "I've never seen you tell someone off like that. What is wrong with you? He's one of my biggest clients!"

"I know," I said, "and I'm sorry. But I just could not take it! He was being rude and ignorant, and I just don't want to be around people like that."

Over dinner, I tried to win this man back, but he was clearly embarrassed, and the relationship between him and Paul was not going to be the same from that point on. I was sorry about the effect it would have on Paul and his business, but I wasn't at all sorry that I'd told this man off. The fact that I'd done it in front of a girl he was trying to impress only made it worse. I wasn't upset about that either.

The next week, I had another run-in, this time with a family member who hadn't been honest about something. I confronted her and told her off, on my moral high horse, all the while wondering why I thought I had any reason to be up there.

I can't remember what it was that eventually made me take a pregnancy test. Like I said, Paul and I hadn't actively been trying for another baby, and since my cycle had been irregular from breast-feeding Bella, I hadn't noticed anything out of the ordinary. But there it was, staring back at me in the form of two distinct pink lines: Pregnant, again. With our third child.

I mourned my need to be in charge of everything.
I had to learn to let go and know it was okay to cry,
to be out of control, to just take the world as it came
and appreciate it, every unpredictable second of it.

CHAPTER 2

Before GiGi's Playhouse,
There Was GiGi

One of the first thoughts I had upon learning that I was pregnant again was that all of my recent moral superiority suddenly made sense. "Paul," I said to my husband, "this baby has a voice! This baby has already changed me for the better. This baby is going to be a world leader or do something great in the world!" Paul rolled his eyes, but I felt it. I was so excited to see who my baby would become. I couldn't wait.

Toward the end of the pregnancy, I started getting preeclampsia and toxemia and losing protein in my urine, so, once again, I spent a lot of time in doctors' offices. The obstetrician determined that everything was fine with me, so the doctors all turned their attention to the baby. They brought in a perinatologist from Loyola, who performed some level-two ultrasounds. Because of the scare we'd had with Bella, I wasn't overly looking forward to the ultrasounds, but everything looked fine. I truly believe that was God protecting me; no test showed any evidence of a problem with the baby. If I had known that something was wrong, I would have been in a complete state of panic.

The day before the baby was born, I went into the hospital to have a blood test. As with Bella, the doctors had been monitoring me carefully because of the possibility that my scar would rupture. They were scheduled to take the baby three weeks before my due date, and the perinatologist wanted to test to make sure the baby's lungs were strong enough. While I was sitting in the waiting room, a little boy with special needs sat nearby, staring at me. I smiled at him and waved. He didn't wave back but kept staring at me in awe and amazement. It was as though he saw something around me. He gasped, his eyes grew wide, and he put his hand to his mouth. He couldn't tear his eyes away from me. I wondered what had made him react that way, and I had a moment of panic that he'd seen something wrong with my baby. *Did my baby just die? Was he seeing an angel come out of me?* I panicked in inward silence. I looked back at the little boy, and all of a sudden, I felt the baby kick. *Thank God,* I thought. *My baby is okay.* I breathed a sigh of relief and smiled again at the little boy, who was still staring at me in awe.

The next day was the scheduled C-section. We showed up at the hospital, calm, cool, and collected. Since Franco's birth had been difficult and stressful, but Bella's had been much easier, I figured this last one would be smooth sailing; at this point, I was an old pro. We knew that, since she was three weeks early by design, the doctors and nurses would take her immediately to the NICU to monitor her lungs and make sure she was healthy, so I was prepared for that. I thought I was prepared for whatever was coming our way.

When we arrived at the hospital at the appointed time, I asked for a private room. We had friends and family in town—the advantage to knowing when the baby is going to be born—and we wanted to create a celebratory atmosphere. Unfortunately, the hospital couldn't give us a private room, but that didn't dampen our festive mood. We laughed and talked with our visitors and the medical staff, all of us joking around. We were excited to meet our new baby.

When it was finally time for the baby to arrive, everything went smoothly. The surgery was quick; the doctor took the baby out, and she cried. I held her briefly, for just a moment, before they took her to the NICU as a precaution. But she looked perfect. She had the same almond-shaped eyes as her older brother and cried the same way her sister had. Finally, our baby was here. We named her Giuliana; we called her GiGi.

After the nurses had taken GiGi to the NICU to monitor her, I lay in the recovery room, happy but exhausted. Time passed, and after a while, I began to wonder where everyone was. Eventually, Paul came back into the room. I knew from the look on his face that something wasn't right. He looked concerned, his brow furrowed.

"What's wrong?" I asked him, a sinking feeling in my stomach.

He shook his head. "There's a lot of people talking about her," he told me. "I don't know what's happening."

I didn't know what Paul knew, or what he had seen. I knew only that I had seen my baby with my own two eyes and held her in my arms, however briefly. And she was fine; she was perfect. Paul sat near the head of my bed and held my hand.

A short while later, the doctors came back. There is no more vulnerable position to be in than lying in a recovery room, having just had a C-section. You can't sit up; you can barely move. So, when the three white coats of my ob-gyn, the hospital neonatologist, and our family pediatrician all entered the room together and stood next to my bed, I felt like I was facing a frightening tribunal. I could feel my heart start beating fast.

"What?" I said, wanting to know everything. "What's wrong?"

The pediatrician cleared his throat. "We ... uh ... we wanted you to know that we've started her on oxygen."

I nodded. *Okay,* I thought. *Is that all? That's fine; we knew her lungs might need some help.*

The neonatologist didn't say anything; she was silent. I looked from her face to my doctor's, and I could tell that wasn't all. Something was wrong. And it was bad. Finally, my doctor spoke.

"We did some tests," he said slowly, "and we think we saw some soft markers for Down syndrome."

As if his words had opened a floodgate, all three doctors began talking at once. I could tell that Dr. Reddy, the pediatrician, was scared but in denial. All around me, the doctors kept talking about further tests and treatments and next steps. I heard nothing. All I could think was that, somehow, I had brought this upon myself. The words of the doctors echoed inside my head as I thought, *What have I done?* Paul was standing behind me, so I couldn't see his face, but I kept picturing his worry, his creased forehead, and his fear. I thought I had willed this on myself. I had always been drawn to children with Down syndrome. It hit me like a shock wave, and I thought back to Joey, the little boy I'd met at the mall whom I had instantly been drawn to and wanted to care for. I thought of my mother, who worked with adults with developmental disabilities. For my whole life, I'd been around Down syndrome; it had become a part of me. Did I do this? People with Down syndrome were always my favorite. Did I somehow make this happen?

The doctors were still talking. I was worried for Paul, and for Bella and Franco. *How will they handle this?* I wondered. I knew I could take it, but what about the rest of my family?

All I wanted was to make eye contact with Paul, to see how he was doing. I honestly had no idea what he was thinking. Finally, Paul came around the side of the bed and took my hand.

"If anyone can handle this, we can," I said.

"Can you imagine what better kids Bella and Franco will be because of her?" Paul said to me.

At the sound of his words, I exhaled, unaware that I'd been holding my breath. *My husband,* I thought, *coming through when I need him most. I didn't see that coming.* I smiled at Paul, squeezed his hand, and turned to the doctors.

"I want to see her," I said, interrupting them.

They paused, midsentence, and looked at me.

"I need to see my baby," I said, wanting to confirm their news for myself.

It took a while for me to get in to see GiGi. The private room we'd been denied earlier in the day suddenly appeared, and we were sequestered in privacy, as though the hospital wanted to keep our misfortune contained, lest anyone else catch it. The hospital staff kept sending in the clergy, every denomination, who all asked, kindly, if we wanted to pray with them. Of course I did, but what was I praying for? I was running out of patience.

"Is she dying?" I asked Paul. I couldn't figure out why else they would be treating us as if we were made of glass and might shatter.

Finally, I was allowed into the NICU to see GiGi. She lay in an isolette, hooked up to an oxygen supply. I studied her face for any of the telltale signs of Down syndrome; I saw nothing. "She has the same eyes as Franco," I said to Paul.

Dr. Reddy nodded. He turned to the other doctors and said, "She looks just like her other babies."

Paul pulled out his wallet and flipped to a picture of Franco as a newborn.

"See?" I said, indicating the picture, "She looks just like her big brother."

The neonatologist shrugged. "Well," she said, "we'll have to do some chromosomal testing to be sure."

That night, I sat in the NICU and held GiGi, bonding with my new daughter. *She's fine,* I told myself. *She's just like her brother and sister. There's nothing wrong with her.* I looked down at her, sleeping in my arms. She stretched, and, in a flash, I saw it. For a brief moment, I saw what the doctors had seen. I saw Down syndrome in my beautiful daughter. My heartbeat quickened. And just like that, it was gone. She settled back into my arms and looked just as she had before, just like Franco, just like a normal baby.

As I tried to breast-feed GiGi—I was told it would be harder—I told myself that if she latched and was able to nurse, the doctors were wrong; they were being paranoid. *We'll show them,* I thought to myself. Just as I'd hoped, GiGi latched right away. She looked up at me, and I thought, *We got this, baby girl. That flash of Down syndrome I saw was just gas! Let it rip!*

As I sat there nursing GiGi in the NICU, the neonatologist approached. She seemed surprised that GiGi was nursing without a problem. She studied us for a minute and checked her watch. She'd been on for forty-eight hours and was about to go home for some much-needed rest, but she was checking in on us one last time. Again, she looked from me to GiGi, nursing hungrily. "I may have been overzealous in my diagnosis," she said, almost apologetically. "We still have to do chromosomal testing to be sure but, uh, I may have been wrong." I nodded, too tired to say much of anything else. She patted my shoulder and left.

It's amazing what you can convince yourself of if you want it badly enough. That whole evening and into the next morning, I ping-ponged between believing that the doctors were wrong—like the shadow on Bella's ultrasound that had turned out to be nothing. Maybe this was just a mistake, a blip that wouldn't matter in the end. Then, I'd segue immediately into knowing with certainty that my new baby girl had Down syndrome, and there was nothing I could do about it. Back and forth, back and forth; all day, I rationalized, begged, reasoned, and questioned. In my heart, I think I knew, but I tried like hell to will away her diagnosis.

GiGi was born on Friday, August 2, 2002. The weekend was one of uncertainty and fear. People came to visit us, as they had when I'd given birth to Franco and Bella, but instead of celebration and laughter, the day was filled with tears and consolation. Just as before, the clergy kept coming in and out, in case we wanted them. Family members, who had not come to visit when I had either of my other children, came to see me the day after GiGi was born. They entered the room crying, tears streaming down their faces.

I just had a baby, I thought. *This isn't how it's supposed to be.*

Whereas with Bella, the delivery room had been a joyful party, after GiGi was born, the staff was silent and stoic. I looked around; no one would make eye contact with me. The medical staff who had been hanging out with us earlier in the day and cracking jokes suddenly became very serious and intent on their tasks. I got the distinct feeling that people were afraid to look at me or talk to Paul and me. The doctors and nurses, while they took excellent care of GiGi and me, consoled me instead of offering their congratulations. They began to treat me differently, looking away and refusing to meet my eye.

Was that extra twenty-first chromosome that defines Down syndrome really that bad? If she had it, would my life, as I knew it, really be over? It sure felt like it by the way I was being treated. I knew that the diagnosis involved low muscle tone and cognitive deficiencies, but I also knew some beautiful things about Down syndrome.

Monday morning, we were packing up and getting ready to bring GiGi home. I walked gingerly down to the NICU, my cesarean scar still tender, and saw that GiGi wasn't there. I panicked. Paul wasn't with me; he'd gone home to get the things we'd need to bring GiGi back with us. "Where's my baby?" I asked a NICU nurse.

She consulted her chart. "They took her down for an EKG," she said. "They thought they detected a murmur."

I slumped down into a chair. At that moment, I knew. I was familiar with the statistics of babies with Down syndrome and the resultant heart problems. I could rationalize all I wanted, but no amount of wishful thinking would change the fact that my daughter was not just like her big brother and big sister. She was different.

I called Paul and told him that GiGi was getting an EKG. Like me, Paul knew what that meant, the implications of it. "Get me out of here," I said to him. "I just want to go home."

After GiGi came back from her EKG, the doctors confirmed the heart murmur. Then, the chromosomal testing came back; they confirmed the Down syndrome diagnosis. Deep in my heart, despite all my rationalizing and denying, I already knew. As much as we try to tell ourselves to think positively, there is a part of us—the part that tries to prevent us from getting hurt—that is always prepared for the worst. That was the part of me that already knew.

Now that GiGi's diagnosis was certain, I felt like the way the doctors and nurses had been acting toward me was justified. Maybe I was being stupid, trying to remain positive. Maybe I was being willfully ignorant.

"I want to take her home," I said to the doctor. "I want to go home."

He looked at me, concern creasing his face. "We need to wait for the results of the EKG," he said.

"I promise I'll bring her back right away," I said. "If she needs to come back, we'll turn right around and bring her back."

The doctor looked me directly in the eye and took a deep breath. "You really shook this place up this weekend," he said.

I had no idea what he meant. Could my tiny new daughter—less than four days old—have really shaken these medical professionals so much? Were they shaken because, with all of their technology, there had been no sign of her diagnosis before her birth? Or were they shaken because they had no idea how to deal with such a diagnosis? They stopped seeing her as a baby the second she was born; they started looking at her as a diagnosis. Maybe it was the 1980s brochure on Down syndrome they gave me. I can tell you it was nothing to celebrate. I didn't know what to do with this information. *Is my life over?* I thought. *I've seen Down syndrome before,* I kept telling myself. *Is GiGi's so much worse than those other cases?* The part of me that was still rationalizing everything thought, *It took you three days to detect it. How serious can it be?*

Out loud I said to the doctor, "I need to take her home."

I began to worry instantly—not about GiGi so much, but about Franco and Bella. If people were already treating me differently, how would they treat them, the siblings of the little girl with Down syndrome? My heart broke for them. I have always hated it when people feel sorry for me, and my children have inherited that trait from me. I wanted nothing more than to protect them. I felt like with GiGi's diagnosis, our family had somehow dropped in stature. We were now "different." We weren't normal anymore. And everyone would be able to tell.

The doctors reluctantly agreed to let us take GiGi home, as long as we promised we'd bring her right back at the first sign of distress. As soon as we walked through the door, I instantly felt better. Away from the beeping machines, the silent nurses, and the atmosphere of dread and foreboding, we were free to be who we were: a family of five with a new baby at home.

That evening, we got the call from the hospital: the results of GiGi's EKG were in. "We need to do more tests as soon as possible," the doctor told me over the phone. "She has two holes in her heart."

Immediately, I could feel my own heart beat faster.

"You don't need to bring her in tonight," the doctor continued, "but first thing tomorrow."

I hung up the phone, feeling devastated.

"Wait a minute," I said to Paul. (Actually, I said, What the hell!?") "This Down syndrome stuff is nothing. I'm okay with that. But I'm not okay with losing her. I can't lose her now."

"You know what?" Paul said, wrapping me in a tight hug. "Fifty percent of kids with Down syndrome have heart issues."

I nodded; I knew this.

"Maybe," he continued, "that's why God does this. It makes the Down syndrome secondary."

I thought about it and realized he was right. Down syndrome is something perpetual, ongoing, whereas a hole in the heart is immediate.

The next morning, we took GiGi back to the hospital for an echocardiogram. To me, her Down syndrome diagnosis stopped mattering while we dealt with her heart issue. Maybe it's because those of us who aren't medical professionals can understand what the heart does, how it works, and even what it looks like; whereas chromosomes are something confusing, invisible, and complicated. All I cared about was fixing GiGi's heart. I needed her to be healthy.

To protect my other children, I vowed not to let them see any negativity around GiGi's birth. I refused to cry in front of them. The doctors wanted to wait until GiGi weighed ten pounds before performing the surgery. Every week, they weighed her on the same scale in the same office, recording her slowly increasing weight. She was having trouble breathing and always had a desperate look on her face. At night, she would sometimes stop breathing. I would literally stand there counting the seconds, praying that she would take another breath. Then, in the dark silence, her loud gasp for air would literally scare the heck out of me. Honestly, it was terrifying.

On the eleventh day after GiGi's birth, we had friends over to the house. We made it celebratory, since the hospital had been such a strange experience for us. A neighbor, who had never been over to our house before, tiptoed over to the bassinet, where GiGi was sleeping, and peered in, almost as if she were afraid. "Oh!" she said, startled. "She's so cute!" She said it as though she were surprised, as if she expected to see nothing but a big ol' chromosome lying in there.

That same day, GiGi had her first experience with heart failure. After everyone left and I went to change her from her clothes into her pajamas, I could see that she was pulling in her chest when she breathed. I called the doctor, and he told us we needed to get her to a pediatric ICU because she was in heart failure. Paul had to stay with Franco and Bella, and I took the panicked ride to the hospital. I brought her in, and I could not get my voice to stop shaking. I controlled my body to take care of her, but my insides were completely freaking out, and it was coming out through my voice. They sensed my panic and immediately grabbed her. I was barely able to get the words out to check her in. They hooked her up to monitors and IVs and put her on drugs to help her heart and relieve the fluid buildup, and then they finally got her stabilized. It was terrifying.

Even with this extra curveball of the heart issue thrown our way, Paul and I bought a new house. I didn't know what else to do, so I went and bought a ten-thousand-square-foot home. To back up a bit, we had planned on building a house and were looking for lots when I was pregnant with GiGi. While checking out a neighborhood we wanted to build in, we saw a house we liked. So, when GiGi was ten days old, we made an offer and bought that house. In some ways, I think it was my way of celebrating GiGi, of not giving in to everyone who was telling us there was something wrong with her. I still hated it when people felt sorry for me, and I thought that if the outside world saw me with this snazzily dressed new baby, this beautiful, amazing house, and these other wonderful, well-adjusted children, they wouldn't feel pity.

In pictures from that time, there is no evidence of bad times or the difficulties we were facing. There are so many pictures of GiGi, with Franco and Bella propping books up in front of her so that she could read—all when she was five days old. I kept everything as light and as joyful as I could while we waited for GiGi to get strong enough for her heart surgery.

When GiGi had her second experience with heart failure, we had gone as a family to do the breast-cancer walk for Giovanna. Because GiGi couldn't be around crowds, we spent some time at the preparty but couldn't do the walk itself. That afternoon, I took GiGi to the doctor to have her weighed again, hoping she would be strong enough for the surgery. After an exam, the doctor determined that we couldn't wait any longer; she was in heart failure again and needed to be hospitalized. GiGi had to have her heart surgery soon. The drugs she was on were not working.

We rode in an ambulance to the children's hospital downtown. The doctor had put GiGi, my tiny baby girl, on the same medications my elderly father was on. She was on a diuretic and something to strengthen her heart. Her other organs had swollen to compensate for her damaged heart. I thought desperately, *We have to wait. I could do it; I could get her up a pound or two so that she'll be stronger.*

When we arrived at the hospital, the doctors met with Paul and I to explain the surgery. Paul's phone rang, and I looked at him, wondering why he hadn't turned it off. He stepped out of the surgeon's office for a moment and when he came back, he said, "We got a cash offer on the house."

Was that a sign? I wondered. Everything seemed to be happening at once. Perhaps the call coming at the exact moment they told us they needed to do GiGi's open-heart surgery felt like a sign from God that He was going to make everything okay: the house would be sold, we would be in our new house, and all would be good. They gave us a date for GiGi's surgery, and we had to come back at the appointed time. The doctor emphasized that the medication she was on was not going to be able to control her heart problems. She needed the surgery.

The night before GiGi's open-heart surgery, I was sitting in our cavernous new house, and I noticed how, in the very short time she'd been a member of our family, she'd managed to take over. There were burp clothes scattered on the living room sofa, bottles cluttering the countertop, and stuffed animals underfoot. This tiny little baby had already taken over our lives and our home. I looked around the house, which was still somewhat unfamiliar to me, and thought, *I could lose her.* It was the first time I had seriously thought that there was a chance that GiGi wouldn't make it. I looked at all the new baby detritus littering our new house, and thought, *If I don't bring her back home, we can't come back here. There's no way I can come back without her.*

When the day arrived, they wheeled GiGi in her tiny isolette down to surgery, and I looked desperately at my brother Joe." "I can get her to weigh more, Joe," I said. "I can do it if they let me have more time." It was my last desperate plea to postpone the surgery, because I was terrified. I couldn't lose her. But they just kept wheeling her away.

Joe rested his hand on my shoulder and said calmly, "You just have to let her go." He told me quietly that a baby with Down syndrome with the same heart issues GiGi had was in the hospital where his wife worked; the baby had just died because she caught a cold. I realized he was right; I wasn't in control. I remember thinking that my family and the doctors were kind to let me think I had some control over the situation but that, in reality, none of it was up to me.

The whole time I waited for the doctors to let us know the outcome of GiGi's surgery, I kept telling myself that I didn't care that she had Down syndrome. I didn't care that she had low muscle tone, or that her brother and sister were going to have to face ignorance and stand up for her. I didn't even care that I had no idea how to do any of this. All I cared about was that my little girl was okay. Thankfully, she was. It was a six-and-a-half-hour surgery that went a little longer than expected, but they successfully fixed both holes. The VSD (ventricular septal defect) was closed with a Teflon patch, and the ASD (atrial septal defect) was sewn shut. I was so afraid of a stitch breaking or the patch lifting, but, luckily it was the only heart surgery she would need.

As GiGi recovered from her surgery, I decorated her crib in the hospital with all kinds of pictures. Like any mother does with her children, I wanted to celebrate GiGi's life. I was determined that her entire life was not going to be about her diagnosis. I put up pictures of GiGi as a daughter, a granddaughter, a niece, a sister. A nurse came in to check on her and seemed surprised to see all the pictures up. Those of us who aren't medical professionals sometimes forget how hard these situations can be on the doctors and nurses who have to deal with them every day. They face emotionally difficult situations all the time. With tears in her eyes, the nurse studied the pictures.

"She's already gone trick-or-treating?" she asked me, indicating a picture of GiGi dressed as a flower, next to her brother and sister in their Halloween costumes.

"Sure," I said. "She couldn't miss that."

The nurse nodded, and I saw her eyes fill with tears. In that moment, all I could think was that she must have had some personal experience with Down syndrome that was making this so difficult on her. Maybe she had terminated a pregnancy of her own. I wanted to ask her, but these things are very private. I also didn't want her to think I was judging her. Still, she stared at the pictures, seeing GiGi as a person rather than a diagnosis. I realized that was the exact reason I had put those pictures up. It was important to me that the doctors and nurses saw my daughter as just that: my daughter. I had to break through the tendency for them to see her as a diagnosis, or a problem to be solved.

Later, a new nurse came in while I visited with GiGi. We had just taken her off the vent when she started moving her head around from side to side. Her eyes weren't focusing. Concerned, I asked the nurse, "Why is she doing that?"

She glanced at GiGi for a moment and watched her methodically move her head back and forth in her crib, with a blank look on her face. "She's fine," she said dismissively.

"No," I said, leaning over GiGi. "She isn't fine. My daughter doesn't do that."

As it turned out, GiGi was having a seizure. This behavior wasn't normal for any child, but because the nurse had just met my daughter, she must have thought this was normal behavior for a baby with Down syndrome. In fact, GiGi was having a seizure as a result of spiking a high fever. All I could think was, *Thank God that I was in the room to be her voice.*

When we finally took her home, I realized something: GiGi was a baby; she wasn't a diagnosis. Just as I had with my other children, I celebrated her life. I dressed her in the cutest outfits I could find because I realized that if people were going to look at us differently, then they were going to see the best-damn-dressed baby around. I flaunted her so that people would be forced to acknowledge her. I didn't want anyone else to be afraid to make eye contact.

And still, I didn't let Franco and Bella see me cry. I did cry, but I did it in the shower or in the car. Those were the places where I allowed myself to feel the flood of emotions, including confusion and anger, that came over me. Everywhere else, I kept it together. But over time, I realized that I wasn't crying because I was mourning the baby I thought GiGi would be; I was crying because I was mourning the life I thought I'd have. This only happened fifteen years ago, but even then, everyone acted as though a Down syndrome diagnosis meant that your life was over. *How can this be?* I thought. *We have plans!* I cried because we were supposed to go to Disney World the Thanksgiving after GiGi was born. I cried because we'd just bought a new house, and I had to decorate it. I cried because, based on everyone else's reactions, I'd never be free again.

I always felt guilty crying. How could I cry about this beautiful baby girl I was holding? How could she not be enough? What was wrong with me that I thought this perfect little person didn't belong in my perfect life? But, eventually, I stopped crying. As GiGi grew and cried and fussed, I realized just how perfect she was. Yes, she had low muscle tone; yes, she would have difficulty doing some things without help—but she wasn't going to break. She wasn't fragile; she was strong. I realized that my life was not supposed to be what anyone else told me it was going to be. Rather, my life was what I was determined to make it. I think I finally realized I didn't mourn GiGi; I mourned my crazy controlling life. I mourned my need to be in charge of everything. I had to learn to let go and know it was okay to cry, to be out of control, to just take the world as it came and appreciate every unpredictable second of it.

No, we didn't get to Disney World that November, but we made it the following March. And since then, we've been able to do everything we've wanted, and more. GiGi hasn't held us back. If anything, she's propelled us forward. Before she was born, even before I knew she was there, GiGi had a voice—as I'm sure my husband's client remembers from that fateful dinner—and her voice has been loud and clear all along, guiding me from the very beginning and continuing to guide me to this day. Through it all, I had to learn to relinquish control and hand the reins to GiGi. She's the one in charge.

*Self-fulfilling prophecy begins in your head and
plays out in your life.*

C H A P T E R   3

*Be Careful What You Wish
For; It Might Just Happen*

I am a big fan of self-fulfilling prophecy. I believe that we all have the power to control the way we feel. Even if I am not feeling good, if someone asks how I am, I always respond positively. I like to send positive, happy vibes because they come right back to me. It's a win-win!

So, when GiGi was born, I was determined to find all the positives in Down syndrome. I remember stopping at the Barnes & Noble when GiGi was just a few days old, and looking for books about raising kids with Down syndrome. I couldn't find anything on the shelves, so I asked the clerk for help.

She punched a few keys on her computer and squinted at the screen. "We don't carry the book in the store," she said. "But if you want, we can order it for you, and it'll be here in three to five business days."

I looked down at GiGi in her carrier. "I don't have three to five days," I said. "I'm raising this baby now!" I wanted to add, "And I am clueless!" But I didn't.

In a lot of ways, that experience was the inspiration for opening GiGi's Playhouse. I did it not only because I wanted to create a place for children with Down syndrome and their families but also because I wanted GiGi to have that kind of place too. I looked around and found support groups and meetings—all doing good work—but none of them offered what I was looking for, and none provided immediate help or support. Eventually, I realized that the place I envisioned didn't exist, and so I would have to create it.

All the places where I could have met someone with Down syndrome were for adults; all the support groups were for the parents. I was looking for a place with kids. Spending time only with parents and adults with Down syndrome seemed distant to me and, honestly, a little scary. Some of those adults were never able to receive the life-changing therapy offered today. I was the mother of a new baby; seeing adults didn't do much to address the needs of my daughter or our family. I wanted to see what my life was going to be like in the future, but all I could see was the *distant* future, when GiGi reached adulthood.

Frustrated, I became a crazy person, and whenever I saw a child with Down syndrome, I became a stalker! I followed closely behind, trying to understand what the next few years of my life might look like. I'm surprised no one ever reported me to the police! But I wanted to be with those parents; I wanted to see those babies, and I wanted to learn from them. I wanted to know what to expect.

Unable to get books that provided the information I wanted as quickly as I needed it, I turned to the internet. This was fifteen years ago. The internet wasn't new, but it wasn't quite the repository of information overload that it is today. Before I found what I was looking for, I had to wade through a sea of awfulness and hateful rhetoric. What's that equation? Anonymity plus a platform equals idiots! That's what I was finding as I searched for information about caring for my daughter. People hiding behind the wall of anonymity that the internet provides talked about "retards" and how they didn't want their kids exposed to "people like that." There was so much hateful, ignorant speech that it sickened me, and I began to feel helpless. Why did people think this was okay? I decided not to dwell in their ugly negativity. I was going to counteract their negativity with positives! In that moment, I knew I needed to change this. I did not want another mother to see this as her first initiation into Down syndrome. I wanted to start GiGi's Playhouse so that we would be the first thing that came up when people searched for "Down syndrome awareness." I couldn't stomach the idea of other parents and families facing an internet full of ignorant opinions. I wanted their first experience to be one of hope and acceptance. I wanted to provide a new perspective, a celebration, a bright spot in that dark place on the internet.

Going back to fifteen years ago, I eventually found myself in a chat room for moms of children with special needs. For a while, I just lurked, reading the other moms' stories. I was new at this and began as a virtual voyeur, reading about other people's experiences and cringing at the problems they faced when dealing with acceptance, treatment, and discrimination. Slowly, I started to contribute my two cents and talk about my experiences. I told them about GiGi's doctors and the reaction from the hospital staff. I wrote about the reactions from people in stores and on the street, describing how people seemed surprised when they saw what an absolutely adorable baby GiGi was. Many of the women in the chat room had similar experiences. They understood where I was coming from.

One day, when GiGi was about five months old, I logged in to the chat room while she napped. A woman was talking about her daughter. She told us that she'd been in a dance class where they were preparing for a recital. She wrote about how the instructor had yelled at her daughter so much that her daughter had started biting her nails out of nervousness. She'd done it so much that her nails were ragged and bleeding. The mother asked if there was a place that our kids could go, where they could dance but wouldn't be so pressured to keep up. She expressed concern that her daughter's dance class was all about appearances, and the instructor demanded perfection. Her daughter, desperate not to fall behind, had become a nervous wreck.

What this woman wrote hit me where I lived, making me think of all the other kids out there who were not being treated properly. I had never met her or her daughter, but I could picture this small girl—only five or six years old—absolutely torn up with nerves and fear, chewing on her fingers until they bled. It was unacceptable, and I wanted to do something about it. *Why would you want your child somewhere where she isn't welcome?* I thought. "You've got to take her out," I said to the mother. "Don't put your kid in a situation where she's not wanted."

"But she loves to dance," she replied. "I just want to find a place where she can dance without so much pressure."

"Actually," I typed, without thinking, "I'm going to open a place like that."

The statement wasn't totally out of the blue. As I said earlier, for a while—ever since GiGi was born—I'd been thinking about a place where kids with Down syndrome and their families could go to celebrate their diagnosis, a place where the kids would be leaders. I wanted a place that was all about self-esteem and acceptance. I wanted it because I wanted GiGi to be a leader. I thought about the voice I'd found when I was pregnant with her, before we knew about her diagnosis, and I realized that this was what she'd been telling me. I looked down at my tiny sleeping daughter and realized that she was already a leader. Now we just had to build her and her friends a stage.

Thinking back, that was a self-fulfilling prophecy slapping me right in the face. You see, a few days before, I was carrying GiGi to her crib and felt her low muscle tone. To clarify, low muscle tone is what makes everything so hard for people with Down syndrome. Even with therapy, it is a lifelong struggle. The low muscle tone is usually what makes people think that individuals with Down syndrome are weak. (I think they assume this because they do not understand that the muscle tone is the root of the problem.) In any case, while holding a sleeping GiGi, I recognized the tremendous weight of her low muscle tone that I'd never realized existed, because her sheer determination and never-ending smile outshone what she had to overcome. I promised her that night that I would change the way the world saw Down syndrome. I had no clue how I would do this, but maybe starting a place like I'd described in the chat room was part of it.

Immediately after my response to the young dancer's mom, the chat room began lighting up with questions. "Where is it going to be?" the other moms asked. "What's it going to be called?" They wanted to know what programs would be offered and how much it would cost. At the time, I had no answers, but once I'd put it out there, I knew I had to do it. I felt a responsibility to these mothers—these kids and their families—even though I'd never met any of them. I felt like I had a community, and they were counting on me. That conversation was exactly the catalyst I needed to get GiGi's started. And so, blindly, acting first and asking questions later, I got to work.

*I realized that the place I envisioned didn't already
exist, and so I would have to create it.*

CHAPTER 4

Creating GiGi's Playhouse

Motivation Starts from Within

From the very beginning, creating GiGi's Playhouse was all about
the kids. At the time, I had just been featured in the local paper, in
a story about early intervention (EI) and therapy for children with
Down syndrome (DS). (I usually spell out *Down syndrome* and *early
intervention,* but I've listed the abbreviations that are commonly used
so that you'll recognize them if you encounter them elsewhere.) In
the article, I talked about my belief that accepting and working with
the diagnosis early was a huge part of ensuring that your child would
be successful. I had spoken about GiGi and the therapies she had

started when she was just three months old. I believed it was crucial to start early, though I certainly understood the struggles other parents faced with accepting the diagnosis. It bears repeating that one of the best things we can do as parents is to begin therapy and intervention early. That makes everything easier. I believe this to be true for any diagnosis.

It may sound overly simplified, but the truth is, the sooner you accept the diagnosis, the better your life will be. Push forward! Allow yourself to see past the diagnosis and look toward the possibilities. My motivation was to find new strategies to help GiGi succeed. To make people have no choice but to see her potential.

There was the moment when I realized how the low tone would affect her fine-motor skills. My other kids were able to pick up Cheerios and find their way to their little mouths. GiGi certainly knew where her mouth was, but picking up those tiny little suckers was a struggle. That damn pincher grip! So, I gave her a little help in the high chair. I put a little broken Pop-Tart on there, which of course would stick to her finger, and then I put her fingers in her mouth. Her eyes lit up! *What the heck was that? It's called motivation, sister! I am not going to put them in your mouth; you are going to work for it.* Next thing I knew, those little fingers were working hard, trying to find a way to do that again. Okay, I know some people would freak about the sugar, but she didn't have any teeth!

The point is, find what works for you, and make it happen. That's my best advice.

There are many obstacles to getting early intervention and therapy. One of them has to do with the parents themselves: they may not see the value, or they may not think their children need it. Sometimes even a therapist will tell parents that a child doesn't need therapy. But the truth is, early intervention and therapy are like going to the gym and working with a personal trainer. That's the analogy I like to give to explain the benefits. Our kids should be getting this therapy early on—and they are entitled to it—but many therapists will say, "Oh, she doesn't need it. She's doing great." But the truth is that we all need a little extra push from time to time. I try to explain it to reluctant parents by saying, "Think about when you go to the gym. If you're going to the gym on your own, you're probably going to get a good workout, right?" They understand that. "But," I continue, "if you're meeting with a personal trainer at the gym and *he's* working you out, your muscles are getting worked in the right way, and you're really focusing on the parts where you need extra help. And that's when you will see change! Think of early intervention and therapy like a personal trainer, just giving your child that extra boost." This often works with parents. Something about considering the intervention and therapy in a new light makes it easier for many of them to accept their children's diagnosis and to understand that the therapy is a boost, a support that will help their kids down the line.

GiGi s Playhouse Down Syndrome Awareness Calendar: Images of Our Beautiful Children

Around the same time that the article appeared, I had planned to have a family picture taken with our new, bigger family—now that GiGi was a part of it. I knew that my daughter was beautiful, and I spent a lot of time and energy finding a photographer who would be able to capture that. Despite all my progress and my preaching, I still sometimes had trouble shaking the mental picture of the portrayal of Down syndrome from the 1950s: black-and-white pic, child with bad hair and his tongue hanging out. I wanted to do better for our kids, and as we got our family picture taken, I thought about doing a calendar. I thought about trying to find a photographer who would understand what I wanted to do. I wasn't interested in hiding the diagnosis; I wanted to celebrate it. I wanted to show these kids with their happiness radiating off the page. I wanted to counteract negativity, and simultaneously help families see the beauty and potential of individuals with Down syndrome. I envisioned it as a counterpoint to the awful 1980s pamphlet the hospital had given me when GiGi was born. *Maybe,* I thought, *if parents got this calendar instead, they would see that there is hope and a much brighter future than they've been told.* I also hoped that the calendar would help parents to accept their children's diagnosis. Maybe even just the fact of the calendar's existence—that someone had taken the time and energy to celebrate these beautiful children—would send the message that their children were already accepted, and it would urge them to become part of that culture of acceptance.

As the photographer snapped the family pictures, with GiGi dressed to the nines and snuggled in my arms, I began to mentally plan the calendar. I knew it could be successful and beautiful; I just had to get it right.

In our area, four children with Down syndrome had been born within four months of each other. Three of us—including our family—lived within one mile of each other. After the newspaper article, some of the other families sought me out. They wanted to meet and share resources. All our kids were the same age, and we were all dealing with the same issues and complications. We met up at a local restaurant.

In the middle of dinner, I brought up the idea of the calendar and the Playhouse, and explained how I saw them supporting each other. I saw the two parts working hand in hand.

"I just thought it would be great if people could see how beautiful our kids are," I said. "I think it might actually really help people to see positive, smiling, confident images."

Immediately, the parents were onboard. They loved the idea. Many of them offered suggestions about where to shoot it or how it should look.

"If you want to be a part of this," I said, "let's do it." I was excited to have their support.

I don't think I realized it at the time, but we had just unofficially formed the first GiGi's Playhouse board. All the parents there that night had a vested interest in the perception of kids with Down syndrome, and they were all passionate about having a place where their kids could be leaders. Like the mother with the daughter who loved to dance, these people loved their children fiercely and wanted a place for them. We set out to make it happen; we decided to change the world.

Of course, I had no idea what I was doing. I knew vaguely that it was going to be a nonprofit organization and that I wanted to provide activities and therapy for children and families free of charge, but that was as far as I had thought it out. Today, when people ask me about the initial business plan for GiGi's Playhouse, I laugh. I didn't have a business plan! What I had was a desire to make a difference and to find people who wanted to help, and the need to do something quickly so that GiGi could benefit. Above all, I believed in miracles, which was probably the most important part of it all.

A few weeks after that dinner, I went to look over the proofs for our family pictures. I looked at GiGi, all dolled up, and thought about what a beautiful daughter I had. *I need more people to see our kids like this,* I thought.

"You know," I said to the photographer, "I'm thinking about doing a calendar of our kids, kids with Down syndrome, for this nonprofit I'm starting." I spoke calmly, casually, gauging her reaction.

"Oh my gosh!" she blurted. "I have always wanted to do something like that!"

"Really?" I asked, looking at her. "You have?"

"Absolutely!" she said.

I glanced through the proofs again. "Well," I said, trying to keep my voice nonchalant. "If you want to submit some of your work, I can show it to our committee."

"That would be amazing!" she gushed. She didn't know that our committee consisted of me, myself, and I. We had no formal structure and no budget. We just had an idea. But I wanted her to value our kids. I wanted her to know them and to understand why this project was important. I don't think I lied to her. I just wanted her to believe that what she was doing was worth it, and if I made her think that other people wanted to shoot the calendar as well, maybe she'd want to do it even more. I figured that a little professional competition—especially if it helped our kids—was a good thing.

She submitted her pictures to me, eager to show off her work.

"I'll let you know what the board says," I told her.

When I went back to pick up the family pictures I had chosen, she seemed nervous. "Did you talk to your board?" she asked timidly.

"Oh yes!" I said, reminded that this woman thought she was in fierce competition with other photographers. "And they chose you!"

She was so excited, she clapped her hands and jumped up and down.

For nine years in a row, Cynthia Frericks, that same amazing photographer, took the pictures for our annual GiGi's Playhouse Down Syndrome Awareness Calendar. GiGi is one of many kids featured in it. Fifteen years later, people still love it! (Even though most of us live by our Outlook calendar these days.) But this calendar is inspirational and sends a beautiful message. And Cynthia did it all pro bono. Even after we had a budget and a business plan, she insisted on donating her time and talent to the calendar. I credit the calendar with a lot of GiGi's success. That old saying that a picture is worth a thousand words is no joke! And the happy, smiling children in our calendar speak much louder than the terrible outdated pamphlets from the hospital. That positivity has always been our goal—it still is.

Designing the Playhouse

As with the calendar, a miracle occurred when I was chatting with a friend about building a stage for the kids. My friend was an interior designer, and I was throwing out ideas about what the Playhouse should look like. "I want to have a place where these kids can be free to perform and get up on stage and be awesome," I said. "I want it to be all about building self-esteem and taking it out into the world." I told her about the little girl who loved to dance but who, out of nervousness and stress, bit her fingernails until her fingers bled. "I want to have a place for her to dance and for her and her family to celebrate her diagnosis."

My friend got a strange look on her face. She was quiet for a moment. Finally, she said, "It's so weird, but I just got this stuff, and I have no idea what to do with it."

"Stuff?" I asked her, curious.

"Curtains," she said. "A high school is redoing their theater, and they just donated their stage curtains to me. I have no idea why I even took them; I had no idea what to do with them." She looked at me hopefully. "Do you want them?" she asked. "I think they'd be perfect."

"Yes!" I said. I was thrilled. All of a sudden, we had stage curtains— real ones. I knew our kids would be thrilled.

Miracles like that kept happening. The stage curtains were a perfect example. We could have just hung up old bedsheets as stage curtains, but it was important to me that our kids weren't treated as an afterthought. I wanted them to have the real thing, not a leftover. It's why I was dead set on *not* setting up our first GiGi's location in a church basement or some other out-of-the-way place where we wouldn't be in anyone's way. I wanted something bigger. I wanted GiGi's to be up front, brightly colored, and the center of attention. "I've been to that place," I said. "That is not what this is." I didn't want our kids to be hidden away, out of sight and out of mind. I wanted people to see them. I wanted their achievements to be public. I wanted people to take notice. "If you put us in a basement," I said, "that sends the message that it's where they belong. It makes it seem like there's something shameful about Down syndrome." That was exactly what we'd been trying to combat with the calendars. We couldn't take a step back now and hide in the basement. The curtains were more than just a decorating detail; they were a symbol. The Playhouse was going to be a real venue, out in the open, out in the light.

Dealing with Logistics

As I was working to get GiGi's Playhouse up and running, I was still a mom raising three kids. At the same time, I was driving my sister-in-law Giovanna to her chemotherapy appointments once a week, caring for her daughter Romi, and trying to get my brother settled into a living situation. I had a lot on my plate, but I've never known a lower gear. And while I'd always known that I'd be doing something like this, I thought that, because of my brother, it would have something to do with mental illness. But when GiGi was born, the focus had to change. In the back of my mind, I think I knew that if I didn't push to get this place started, no one else would.

I began talking to Paul about the worries and fears I had about starting a nonprofit. The idea of the Playhouse had started to crystallize in my mind, and I knew that, above all, I didn't want to charge people for anything. "The last thing these people need is to worry about paying for this," I told him. "If we charge money, a lot of the parents will use it as an excuse to not give their kids the treatment they need."

Accepting the diagnosis is hard, and moving forward to get your child the care he or she needs is immensely difficult. I didn't want to make it easier for parents to make excuses.

"The kids need a place like this," I emphasized. "And it has to be free."

Paul agreed that it was important, but he was also cautious. All along, I had wanted to have four children. Paul had always known this. But he could see the toll that raising three kids and trying to start a nonprofit was having on me. Three young children are a lot for any mother to handle, but when one of those children has Down syndrome, is breast-feeding, and is in therapy four times a week, it's that much harder. Plus, Giovanna was still going to chemotherapy every day, and we were struggling to get my brother settled as well. There were days when I would think, *This cannot be my life.* From waiting in the school line to pick up the kids, to chemo, to baseball, to therapy, to chasing my brother down the street with the police, to dance, then dinner—was just another day.

"If we do this," Paul said, "we can't have another kid. We just can't do it."

I looked down at GiGi and realized he was right. I swallowed hard and agreed with Paul. I decided that the Playhouse would be my fourth child. I told myself that instead of raising another child, I'd help to raise hundreds more by providing them with a place where they could learn and be leaders.

"Okay," I said to Paul. "No more kids."

(Of course, as a self-fulfilling prophecy would have it, I would eventually end up with a fourth child when we adopted Romi after Giovanna died in March 2005. It was not what I had expected, but there was no way—even with all we had on our plate—that we weren't going to make Romi part of our family. She's made us stronger and better than we ever would have been without her. But I have learned that I should be careful what I wish for. I wanted four kids, and I got them—and so much more!)

Meanwhile, Paul continued. "There's something else. It's great that you want to open up this place and let the world come for free, but we have to protect ourselves."

He was right, of course. I thought about what would happen if a kid fell and got hurt at the Playhouse. At the time, it was all our personal finances tied up in the Playhouse; we needed protection. I didn't relish calling the insurance company because I had enough experience to know that people see a red flag when you say the words "Down syndrome." Your liability skyrockets. The concern is not warranted, but it's how people feel, and I knew I'd have to be careful.

And that's when the miracles *really* started to happen.

Miracles in Many Forms and in Many Unexpected Ways

Throughout the process of founding GiGi's Playhouse, a lot of things happened in much the same way as the calendar and stage curtains came about. I'd have an idea, mention it to someone, and, somehow, something would happen to make it a reality. I consider that the manifestation of a miracle. The founding of GiGi's Playhouse thereby became a self-fulfilling prophecy for me. In fact, miracles happened every day. I learned that if I put positivity and positive intentions out into the world, something would happen to make good things come true. You've heard of the road rising up to meet you? That's how I felt throughout the process of starting GiGi's. I know that many people will say things like "Well, you were lucky"; or, "You were in the right place at the right time." There is certainly some truth to that, but I believe 100 percent that everything happens for a reason and that I was in the right place at the right time because I was *supposed* to be there. I believe that throughout all of this, miracles—both large and small—kept happening to propel us forward. I even believe that some of the things that seemed like huge hurdles at first—the attitude of many of the medical professionals, for example—ended up being miracles in their own right. Had I not been faced with negativity and frustration when GiGi was born, I might not have doubled down on my intention to make a place for our kids a reality. Everywhere I looked, I saw miracles.

Honesty Is the Best Policy

I suppose I could say that my honesty got us our insurance policy, but, really, it was just another one of the miracles I've been describing. When I called our insurance company, I learned that our usual agent was out of town. I was a little apprehensive about talking to someone else, but I knew I couldn't put this off any longer.

"Oh," I said to the agent who took my call, "maybe you can help me."

"What are you looking for?" he asked.

I was vague, avoiding the use of the words *Down syndrome.* "I want to start a center for kids with special needs," I said. "Sort of an achievement center. A place where they can be leaders."

"So, a school?" he asked. "You want to start a special-needs school?"

"No," I said. "It's not a school." I was getting frustrated. It was difficult to talk about what I wanted without actually saying it. *Screw it,* I thought. "It's a center for kids with Down syndrome," I blurted out.

There was silence on the other end of the line.

After a moment, the agent spoke again. "My son is sixteen and has Down syndrome," he said. "Will there be anything there for him?"

And just like that, our insurance was covered. Another miracle had taken place, and GiGi's Playhouse was getting closer to becoming a reality.

The Business Details: Setting Up an LLC and a 501(c)3

At that time, I knew that if GiGi's was ever going to jump out of my head and into the real world, I had to get serious about obtaining our LLC designation. I filled out all the paperwork and mailed it in, and when I eventually got the legal paperwork back in the mail, I was so excited. I had gotten an embossed certificate with a seal and everything! It looked so legit! I thought I'd made the big time. Of course, at this point, the official GiGi's business plan was still in my head. There was simply no time to put it on paper! Plus, I did not want to hear that it was not possible. So, I faked it all the way through, *as if* I actually had an elaborate plan.

Paul was a commodities trader, and I had been bugging him to ask some of his friends to be on the board, to lend us some legitimacy with planning and to give us money!.

"Nancy," Paul said, "you have to make this a tax write-off for my friends, or they won't do it."

I had learned that in order to be a true 501(c)3, I had to have a real board that consisted of more than just me, my husband, and my parents. In desperation, I started calling people and begging them to be on my board.

"It doesn't matter how much our friends love GiGi and support us," Paul said. "They're just not going to throw money at a business that isn't going to charge a penny and has no revenue stream."

He was right, but what did I know? I hadn't gone to business school!

I called the mother of GiGi's best friend, Jessica, and asked if I could list her husband as our treasurer. He agreed to serve as treasurer, but, to this day, he still jokes that he's waiting for check number 001. "It's probably at the bottom of one of Nancy's purses!" he always says. Which I am sure it is. Luckily, he trusted me, and he knew financial rewards were never my motivation.

I called all my friends and any parents I could think of who had expressed a willingness to help. We had been meeting regularly and talking about what kind of place we wanted GiGi's Playhouse to be, but we still didn't have a formal business plan or board in place. Even though people were supportive, I think a lot of them thought the whole thing was unrealistic or too good to be true.

Start the Presses   Creating Promotional Materials

At the time, when I began pulling together the materials we would need to open GiGi's Playhouse, I knew absolutely nothing about technology. GiGi herself was about seven or eight months old, still breast-feeding and going to therapy four times a week. I was still taking Giovanna to chemo, as well as driving Franco to baseball and Bella to preschool and dance. It was a crazy time, and I was also reaching out to as many organizations as I could to join me on this journey and collaborate. I did not want to reinvent the wheel.

One day, I was supposed to meet this amazing, well connected, Irish guy from a special rec organization that worked with Special Olympics. I was so excited, but the day started out crazy. Franco had soccer camp and couldn't find his pads; Bella had gotten into my makeup while I was breast-feeding GiGi. I was screaming out commands from the chair in GiGi's room, where I was feeding her, desperate to get her to go back to sleep. When it finally happened, I did the army crawl out of her room so that she wouldn't wake up, cleaned up the makeup, and found Franco's pads. A sitter arrived for Bella and GiGi, and I ran out the door, with Franco in tow, grabbing two candy bars for breakfast! Friends lovingly refer to the details of this type of day as a "Nancy story." What can I say? That's just how I roll!

I dropped Franco off at camp and was on my way to my first big meeting when I realized I had forgotten to brush my teeth. So, I stopped for gas, went inside, bought a toothbrush and toothpaste, and brushed my teeth in the gas-station bathroom. Yes, I know, it was pretty gross. Anyway, I ran out of there, got in my car, and went to pull away when something crashed out in front of my car. I thought it was a bird or something crashing down, and I looked at the guy next to me. We were both a little freaked, and then I saw his eyes look around, and he just put his head down. I think he was trying to save me the embarrassment of making eye contact with him, as I realized I had just ripped the gas hose off the pump! I still haven't lived that one down. All in the name of fresh breath.

The meeting was fantastic! I broke the ice by telling him my gas station adventure and we both had a good laugh, and it helped pull me out of my panic of being late. He knew many people in the special needs community and gave me some good connections and sound advice. Nobody was doing what I wanted to do, especially for free, so he encouraged me to get the word out and not to worry about people who didn't get it. He had been serving this community for years, and no matter how hard he tried there were always people who thought they could do it better.

I hadn't worked since Franco was born (1995), and when I did work, I had a production team who did most of the computer work for me. So, I hadn't spent much time learning about technology or computers. I didn't know how to write a letter on the computer or how to create a brochure. I didn't know the difference between a PDF and a JPEG, and I certainly didn't know about graphic design. I was completely in the dark. What I did know was that, if GiGi's was going to be a success, I had to publicize it somehow. We had to raise money for our first location and for our programming, and I knew that there was no way we'd be able to do that without publicizing our message.

The only thing I had was American Greetings Create-A-Card Spiritual Expressions software, a software suite designed to help you create greeting cards and holiday letters. I didn't know anything about editing suites or desktop publishing, and I didn't know anyone who could give me technical help and point me in the right direction. I couldn't share what I'd done, since everything lived in the software program on my computer. The only way to get someone else's feedback on the brochures or letters was to print them out and mark up a physical copy. What a total waste of time! But I didn't know what else to do. I remember nursing GiGi, holding her with one hand while hunting and pecking with the other hand to type up a brochure in that damn American Greetings software. Talk about multitasking!

I needed the brochure because we had set up a table at an event to advertise our first GiGi's location. The first brochure was such a hassle to create. I kept bringing the file to Kinko's so that they could print it out for me, and the file refused to behave. Everything shifted every time they opened it, and nothing would print straight. At the time, you had to pay twelve dollars to bring a disk to Kinko's so that they could turn your file into a PDF. (I am serious here! PDFs were a nightmare back then. Be grateful, people!) Then, they'd print it from the PDF. But every time I brought in the disk, something wouldn't work. I was wasting time and money on uncooperative files.

Finally, I gave in and bought an HP printer for myself. I decided that if the professionals couldn't do it, I'd do it myself. I refused to have an amateur-looking brochure for GiGi's, but I also knew that I couldn't afford to pay someone else to design and print it. So, there I was, breast-feeding GiGi with one hand and feeding sheets of paper into the printer with the other. I made a thousand copies of the brochure, printing them each individually and flipping the paper over to print on the other side. We got them done because we had to; there was no other option.

Eventually, another miracle occurred, and solutions to my technology needs started to fall into place. Someone had mentioned Microsoft to me, and I knew vaguely that they made computer stuff. One day after the opening, tired from having to print out endless copies of a brochure, I called Microsoft.

"I have a nonprofit for kids with Down syndrome," I explained, "and I'm wondering if you could donate some software to help us with our brochures and newsletters."

The person who'd taken my call explained, "There's a process for requesting donations." He told me that I'd have to fill out a bunch of forms and request a nonprofit donation. I knew I didn't have that kind of time—this was a one-woman shop I was running, often with only one hand!

"Thanks," I said, ready to hang up. "I barely have time to breathe, though."

"Wait a minute," he said, stopping me.

"Yeah?" I said.

"I might have a few extra copies of the software in a closet somewhere," he said. "If they fell into the mail, well, I couldn't really do anything about that."

I was confused. I thought he was telling me that he couldn't donate, but that I could buy a software license if I wanted to.

"No thanks," I said. "I was wondering about a donation."

"Right," he told me, emphasizing his words. "I'm saying that if a few copies *fell into* the mail, they might find their way to you, and you wouldn't have to pay for them."

"Oh!" I said, catching his drift. I gave him my address.

Just like that, a complete stranger at Microsoft sent us some free software licenses. I'm sure that he could have gotten in trouble for doing what he did, but I will always be grateful to him for bending the rules for us.

When the licenses arrived, I still had no idea what I was doing. I was still pretty overwhelmed, but there was no denying that even the rudimentary first brochures made with Microsoft Publisher looked way better than anything I'd created with the American Greetings software. One of the things I did learn while messing around with the new software was how much fun it is to teach yourself how to create things on your own. I was blown away by how nice our materials looked when I used real professional tools.

One Sunday afternoon, I got home early from a Down syndrome conference, and with a rare opening in my schedule, I sat down for six hours and created our first newsletter. For five years, that newsletter served as our template. I'm sure it wasn't technically right—and it was far from perfect—but I had done it myself, and I was proud of it. I realized it was important to do two things: (1) not take no for an answer and (2) figure out a way to get each thing done. In a way, we co-opted the Nike slogan to "Just do it," because if something needed to be done, we found a way. Or, perhaps I should say, with miracles and help, things always got done.

October Opening: From Dream to Reality

From the beginning, my goal had always been to open our first Playhouse location in October, for Down Syndrome Awareness Month. October was only a few months away, and we still had no location. I had been making noise around town and had finally gotten our 501(c)3 nonprofit designation, but there wasn't much movement on finding us a location.

One day, I got a call that Bill McLeod, the mayor of Hoffman Estates (the Chicago suburb where the first Playhouse was built), had agreed to meet with me. I had all the neighborhood kids over at the time, and I was so scattered that I realized I didn't have any business cards to make me look legit. I let the kids trash the house while I whipped them up. (Another "Just do it!") Paul came home to chaos, and three minutes before I flew out the door to head to the meeting, I printed the first of my business cards from my own HP printer. I was still tearing apart the perforations and shuffling the cards as I got into the car, hoping like hell that the ink was dry.

The mayor had no idea I had just made those cards. He greeted me warmly, took my card, and asked me to tell him about our plans for GiGi's. To this day, I have no idea how I convinced him that I knew what I was doing. He seemed to have the impression that we were much further along than we were—and I let him believe that. He thought we had amassed a lot of funding, had a great support system, and had an experienced board in place. He seemed to believe in what we were trying to do, so I nodded and smiled and told him about all the programs we were planning for GiGi's once we found a location.

The mayor was particularly receptive to our mission of global acceptance and the goal of GiGi's because he had a daughter who was deaf, and so he had experienced some of the issues faced when a family member had special needs. He understood the importance of having a community of support and the struggle faced when fighting for acceptance and inclusion. He was wholly positive and wished us the best of luck with the opening of GiGi's. He also suggested that I meet with a village planning committee to find a location.

I thanked him, told him I was grateful for his support, and took the information for the village planning meeting. Later, I drove to the address the planning committee had suggested. As I approached, I looked around at the area and the declining state of all the buildings, and my heart sank. *Great,* I thought, *they want to shove us away behind some warehouse. This is where everyone thinks we belong.*

I drove around, surveying the dilapidated location and the papered-up windows on the nearby businesses. I could see that the location was available because it was in a run-down area of town—someplace no business would want to be. I started feeling sorry for myself, wondering why no one could see the potential in what we were trying to do. Why didn't anyone want us to be in the center of the community? It felt like people were trying to hide us, to keep us out of sight. Even the most well-intentioned people who understood that Down syndrome was not a death sentence often felt that it was unpleasant, and they didn't want to have to be forced to deal with the reality of it every day, passing a GiGi's location on their way to get their morning coffee. Yet that was exactly what I wanted the Playhouse to be. I wanted to be part of the community, not separate from it. I looked around at the dilapidated, neglected location, and I fought back tears, thinking of our kids trying to build up their self-esteem in a place like that.

I know I've said this before, but it's so important it bears repeating. Part of my desire to have GiGi's and our kids in the middle of town was that I knew that if people could see these kids wearing their diagnosis on their faces, yet being happy and energetic and active and successful and just bursting with self-esteem, it would inspire others to be more grateful for their own gifts. I've seen it happen before. The hope was that by placing GiGi's someplace where it could not be ignored, people would see our kids, smile, and stop in with their own children to learn. I knew firsthand from my experience with Franco and Bella that exposing your kids to others and teaching them acceptance and inclusion at an early age is key. I knew I wasn't going to find that in this neglected location.

Discouraged, I turned to leave and noticed a Jaguar a short distance away. *What's a car like that doing here?* I wondered. I walked a bit closer, curious. When I got close enough to see the license plate, I smiled. It read "Butera." I knew whose car that was! Johnny B. was a friend of mine. He was an attorney, and his family owned a number of grocery stores and businesses in the area. We'd known each other for a while.

John came out of a nearby building and saw me loitering by his car. As he approached, he recognized me and smiled.

"Johnny B.!" I said. "What are you doing here?"

He gestured to the building behind him and explained that he was working with an architectural printer for one of his locations.

"What are *you* doing here?" he asked. He took one look at my face and asked, "What's the matter? What's going on?"

I explained my situation to him and that I was trying to find a suitable location for the inaugural Playhouse. I told him how everyone kept telling me to put the Playhouse in an out-of-the-way location, a free room, or a church somewhere. "I just feel like everyone wants to hide these kids," I said. "No one wants them to be out there, in the open, for everyone to see."

John was quiet for a second, and then he said, "Why don't you put it in one of my centers?"

"What?" I asked, surprised. I hadn't expected that. I was just venting to a friend.

"I'm serious. There's an opening in a great spot in a great location," he told me. "It's three miles west of Woodfield shopping mall."

I couldn't believe what he was saying. That was right down the street from one of the largest shopping malls in the Midwest! John's location was seen by hundreds of thousands, of people every day. There was a great energy about the place, and lots of foot traffic. It could not have been more different from the run-down area we were in.

"That would be awesome!" I said, hugging John.

I couldn't get over the unexpected generosity I'd stumbled upon yet again. Here I was, feeling sorry for myself and our kids, and out of nowhere, we'd been offered a beautiful location in an amazing area. I knew that with the location John offered, GiGi's would have an even greater chance at success. People would see our location, see our kids, and be drawn in by the activity and excitement. This was *exactly* what I had been looking for. I couldn't wait to get started.

Another day, another miracle. I started to realize that when you're with people who look for miracles, they're even more amazing. If it hadn't been for my chance meeting with John, we might never have secured the fantastic location for the first GiGi's Playhouse. If we'd had to settle for some lesser location where we would have been easier to ignore, I think we'd still be fighting to get our kids included in things. Had we settled and allowed ourselves to be relegated to a basement or shunted to a disused strip mall, we'd still be struggling harder for acceptance. But a miracle happened, and a friend came through when I least expected it. I couldn't have asked for more.

Raising the Funds

Even with the location secured, we still needed to raise a considerable amount of money. There was still a lot of work to be done. Up until that point, GiGi's had been financed primarily by Paul and me; we put up our own money whenever we needed to print brochures, buy supplies, or pay for licenses. We both knew this wasn't a sustainable business model; we couldn't fund a free nonprofit by ourselves. We were also still struggling with taking care of Giovanna—who continued her chemo treatments every Thursday—and settling my brother into the condo we'd just purchased for him because we'd been looking for a place where he'd fit in as well. Both of those things took physical, emotional, and financial tolls on us. We needed help with GiGi's.

We had a party for GiGi's first birthday in August, and we used the event as a huge fundraiser for the Playhouse. We of course invited our family and friends, but we also invited neighbors, colleagues, therapists, board members, and anyone we could find who was interested in helping us build the first GiGi's Playhouse. I figured, *What better way for people to see what the Playhouse was all about than to celebrate with the amazing little girl who had inspired it all?* The party was a huge success, and we raised twenty-five thousand dollars for the build-out of the first Playhouse location—never mind that it cost us ten thousand dollars to throw the party! Little by little, miracles kept happening to make GiGi's a reality.

Nevertheless, we faced a big-time crunch. Remember I was dead set on opening for Down Syndrome Awareness month in October, even though I knew it was going to be tight. People still kept asking me why I didn't wait until GiGi was older to start something like this. People saw me raising three children, and while they admired what I was trying to do, they thought I had too much on my plate. Most of them weren't shy about telling me so. "Wait until she's older," I heard almost daily. "You'll have more time to focus on getting the Playhouse up and running. Just be her mom right now."

I understood why they said that, but what I couldn't make people understand was that if I waited, GiGi wasn't going to benefit from the Playhouse at the time in her life when she most needed it. That's the thing about being the first one through the wall with something revolutionary: A lot of the times, it's the people right behind you who reap the benefit. I didn't want that to happen to GiGi; I didn't want her to miss out on anything. So, I had no choice but to push forward.

I knew that I could have put the Playhouse aside and focused solely on GiGi. I could have spent all my time teaching and tutoring her and doing more therapy; I could have made her a prodigy. If I had done that, GiGi might've become the best violinist with Down syndrome or the best expressionist painter with Down syndrome. She might even have become the best three-star chef with Down syndrome. But I knew that if I did that, I would only be changing GiGi's life, not the lives of other kids. I also wouldn't be able to make the changes necessary to create the future I wanted for her: a world of global acceptance only possible through the Generation G movement we sought to create. Put differently, if only one child does well, it doesn't change perception or open up opportunities for people like GiGi. I didn't want GiGi to be famous for having Down syndrome and being great at one thing. I didn't actually care about her being famous at all. I just wanted her to have positive self-esteem and be able to do everything she wanted to do.

I thought about the woman whose daughter had bitten her fingernails until her fingers bled. I thought about the families who received the same dispiriting pamphlet at the hospital that we had been given. I knew we needed to do better for those kids and those parents. Waiting around for someone else to do it wasn't something I was going to let happen. Gandhi said, "We need not wait to see what others do." I took that message to heart. We had to do it; no one else was going to do it for us.

I realize that not everyone has the time or resources required to put a child in special classes and therapy programs. And not everyone wants to push a kid to excel at something just to prove that the child can do it. I didn't want parents to have another excuse to not accept their children's diagnosis, thinking, "Oh, that's not the kind of Down syndrome my kid has." I wanted them to know that we were there for *everyone,* not just the piano and sculpture prodigies. Don't get me wrong. Being a prodigy is great. But it's not realistic for most people. I remember speaking to a mother who had an absolutely amazing daughter with Down syndrome. Her name is Christine. I watched this girl and thought, *She must be high functioning.* Back then, I thought that was something you were "lucky" enough to have happen to your child with Down syndrome. Now I know that none of us are high functioning or low functioning. That is really a label that is not fair. I know that Christine is who she is by lots of hard work and perseverance. To this day, she works out every day, practices all of her amazing skills, and is one of my best friends. In fact, we call her the seventh Gianni!

"Her IQ isn't higher than anyone else with Down syndrome," Christine's mother explained. "It's just what she's been exposed to."

Parents want their children to reach for the sky, and if we give them the room, they'll do it. But first, parents must truly believe in their children and their future! Here again is something so important it bears repeating: I have never wanted GiGi to be famous for having Down syndrome. I have simply wanted her to be the best she can be, and in doing so, to serve as a *realistic* role model for others. And the only way she can do that is by being herself and being the awesome, energetic, inspiring teacher she is.

The bottom line is that what we really wanted to do with GiGi's Playhouse was to give these kids the opportunity to be kids. I know there are parents out there who say things like "My kid can't tie her shoes, but she can play concert piano!" Personally, I prefer my daughter to be able to tie her shoes. We wanted these kids to be able to become leaders on their own—with support—and to explore all the things they cared about and loved. We wanted them to develop self-esteem and be positive examples to others.

For parents, GiGi's is a place where they can dream and make their dreams for their kids come true. It's a place where they can find the help and support they need. I wanted to provide a place where people could come in and get what they needed. I wanted to give them a place to dream and a platform to help those dreams come true. It's everything to these parents. I know; I'm one of them. I kept thinking, *What would I want for GiGi?* And then, I'd try to build that place. That was the only way to do it. I let my love for my daughter be my guide. I had no instruction manual. And that's why I did all the hard work to create GiGi's, enduring all the craziness and juggling of my own family responsibilities. Because, at the end of the day, it was, still is, and always will be about doing everything to ensure that my daughter's future, and the future of *all* our children, is as bright and full of potential as it can possibly be.

Our Beautiful Website, My "Thanks You" Gift

With the location set, the brochures under control, fundraising under way, and the October opening actually seeming feasible, another miracle soon manifested. I was visiting with a friend at our lake house one day—the same friend who had given us the beautiful stage curtains—and she sheepishly told me that she'd made something for me.

"What do you mean?" I asked her, curious.

She pulled out her laptop and clicked over to a website. "I've been playing around with building you a website," she said. "I mean, for the Playhouse."

I scrolled through the site she'd designed. I could hardly believe it; it was beautiful! In 2003 you couldn't just hire a web designer on Craigslist. Squarespace.com didn't exist, and you couldn't teach yourself web design in a few hours. And yet, my friend had created this website, completely on her own. I was blown away. Remember I was still printing out business cards three minutes before rushing out the door! I had no idea how to build a website. Nevertheless, she'd presented me with an amazing one.

"This is fantastic!" I told her, excited.

"It's weird," she said, clicking through the page, "but I'm a creative, you know. I'm not good with words. But I started doing this, and it was like I could feel my mom's hands on my shoulders." My friend's mother had passed away years before. She went on: "I was typing fast, and the words just kept coming. It felt like a miracle."

I scrolled through the site. She had put up pictures of our kids smiling and laughing. I smiled myself, looking at what she'd put together. It truly was a miracle.

At the bottom of the page, she had written, "Thanks you!" I clapped my hand over my mouth, and gasped. She looked at me strangely. I pointed the typo out to her.

"Oh, I can fix that," she said. "I was typing fast." She made a move to fix the mistake.

"No!" I blurted out. "Oh my God!" I could hardly believe what

I was seeing. "No, you don't get it! This is my thing! I always write that!" I'd found that whenever I went to type something related to the Playhouse and meant to write, "thank you," my fingers always changed it to "thanks you." I thought it was a sign. It meant that miracles truly were happening, and it was God's way of showing me that I had to keep going, that I had so many people to thank, and that a simple, singular *thank-you* would never be enough. I never noticed it while I was typing, only when I was reading things back, and now it had happened to someone else. This was a sign that the miracles were spreading. This wasn't just about me anymore; the movement was growing. It's true that I was working my butt off, but that small slip of the hand by my friend who had created something wonderful for us out of the goodness of her heart let me know that there was so much more going on than I was even aware of.

"You have to keep it," I said. "Thanks you! It's perfect!"

She left it alone.

There were more miracles, and for each one I say a heartfelt "Thanks you!"

Our Mission at GiGi s

Initially, I had envisioned that GiGi's Playhouse would be the kind of place that any group could use at any time. I envisioned the location being paid for 24-7, and I didn't want a wasted moment. I thought maybe Tuesday could be the day for the autism group to use the location at night, and then Wednesday, the multiple sclerosis group could meet. I wanted a place that was open to all. But the specific focus on Down syndrome was important to me because I had experienced how difficult it was to get GiGi treated as a unique person, not a disability.

"Special needs" often lumps individuals together, and people have a tendency to treat all people with special needs as being the same. They treat them as though they're fragile, like they're going to break. But the bottom line is that all children with special needs are not the same. They have different issues, and they require different therapy and support. I believe that in order for us to get the care and support we need, we have to treat people as unique individuals. That starts with recognizing the difference between the diagnoses. Down syndrome is the largest chromosomal disability in our country and the least funded. It still blows my mind that this is true, but it is.

Twenty-five years ago, cancer was largely viewed as a singular thing. If you wanted to make a donation, you usually wrote a check to the American Cancer Society and trusted that the money would go toward the general good. But, today, you can donate to organizations that specialize in breast cancer, prostate cancer, uterine cancer, lung cancer, or many other specific types. By allowing people to donate to and engage with an organization that most directly affects them, their family, or their loved ones, more targeted research can be done. It's more efficient, and greater medical strides can be made. The same is true with the special-needs population.

This was part of why I wanted GiGi's to be open to everyone but to focus specifically on Down syndrome. When I started talking about it to the community, I realized how much people didn't know. I ran into people who were concerned about building a ramp for wheelchairs.

"Wheelchairs?" I said. "Who has wheelchairs? Our kids aren't in wheelchairs any more than the typical population."

Of course, there are some children with Down syndrome who will need to use wheelchairs, but there are just as many typical children who break their legs playing soccer and need to use wheelchairs. Our kids didn't need them more than other kids did.

I realized that a lot of people's assumptions came from unfamiliarity with the diagnosis. People didn't (and usually still don't) understand that our kids have low muscle tone, which makes it harder for them to learn things—particularly physical things—but that, eventually, they learn them. People assumed that Down syndrome was a handicap that required ramps and accommodations for people with disabilities. That was when I understood education was going to be needed. People didn't know what they were dealing with, and it was going to be our job to teach them.

The goal of GiGi's had many facets: education, global acceptance, inclusion, community awareness, and more. First and foremost, the focus on Down syndrome was paramount. In advance of our opening, I reached out to local support groups for help. We needed help in getting the word out to families, notifying them that we were opening and would be providing free programming. GiGi was only a baby, and I did not know many families of kids with Down syndrome at all. But I knew they were out there, and I was building the Playhouse for them as much as for GiGi. That was a mixed bag, because I quickly learned that a lot of nonprofit groups don't like other nonprofits that have new ideas and a new way of thinking. Many of them felt that they'd done things the same way for years and there was no reason to change. I can't blame them; I understand. But I had envisioned GiGi's as a place for community where all people could feel they had a home that had been paid for and that involved a new way of thinking.

However, as we worked toward opening, and I had more discussions with various groups, I began to realize that people had smaller and different dreams. A lot of the groups didn't care about the larger community; they cared about their group. They weren't interested in working with an organization fostering Down syndrome acceptance worldwide, because they were focused on their own group. It didn't make sense to me. I didn't understand why we all couldn't support each other. We weren't reinventing the wheel or repeating services, so why couldn't we work together? I was looking to build on what they had accomplished, not negate it. As I saw it, there was plenty of room for all of us under the tent of acceptance. I wanted go forward together. In fact, I envisioned the Playhouse being given to the Down syndrome groups. I felt that it was theirs to use as they wanted, and I would just fund it and take part in the programs. It seemed God had a different idea!

We re Almost There

The opening of the first GiGi's location garnered some local press, and we were being talked about as the voice of today for Down syndrome. We wanted to share that voice with the entire community—including the community of Down syndrome advocacy, research, and support groups. Some of the established groups were afraid, calling us exclusionary or saying that we weren't being realistic in our goals. As with everything, you have to take the good with the bad, but we genuinely do try to include these groups, inviting them to visit our Playhouses and see for themselves the work we're doing. It's still a struggle.

The whole opening was a struggle, a labor of love. The date for the opening kept getting pushed back for a number of reasons, including the fact that the permitting and zoning meeting was a nightmare. I went to a permitting meeting to explain to the committee what we were planning to do with GiGi's.

The village attorney could not grasp the goal of a place like GiGi's. "There's nothing like this anywhere across the country," he kept saying. "We've looked into this, and for people like that, nothing exists."

"I know that," I said. "That's why we're starting it."

"For these kind of people, we have no model to base this on," he said. He kept using different pronouns to describe us. He kept using phrases like "people like them" and "those kind of people" when referring to people with Down syndrome. It was hurtful and discouraging, but it drove us forward.

"I'm just not sure how we'd zone for a place for people like that," he said.

That was it! I was fed up. "Look," I said, standing up and speaking loudly, "when I go to a restaurant with my daughter, I don't have to sit in the Down syndrome section. The restaurant is zoned for everyone!" That got his attention. But I had made my point. Yes, GiGi's Playhouse was created to support people with Down syndrome and their families, but its larger message was about inclusiveness and acceptance for all. We weren't going to kick out typical children who wanted to come in and see what was going on! In fact, we would be inviting the entire community in.

Finally, we got our permit. I felt like I had jumped through hoops to convince the zoning board that we weren't going to be handling toxic waste or building a crack house. We just wanted a place for kids to be able to grow and learn and become leaders, all while celebrating their diagnosis. It wasn't dangerous, and it wasn't risky. Why couldn't people see that?

I'd like to say that these are fights we don't have anymore. And while we have them less often, there are still people who throw up roadblocks because of their ignorance about Down syndrome. But with every child and every location, we chip away at that prejudice bit by bit.

Despite all the delays, I was still adamant that we open during October for Down Syndrome Awareness Month. I didn't care if we opened at midnight on Halloween; I just wanted it to be in October. Finally, we chose a date during the last week of October. Of course, me being me, I kept piling more stuff on my plate the week before the opening. Franco had started first grade that September, and Bella was in preschool. GiGi was still in therapy four days a week, and on top of that, our house had been featured on a house-walk tour of our neighborhood, so we had people tramping through the house over the weekend. I was also still driving Giovanna to chemo once a week, helping with her girls, and struggling to get my brother into a place where he could feel safe. It was an absolutely insane time.

Days before our scheduled opening, the location was still a mess. There were electrical cords running all over the place because we were "borrowing" electricity from the chicken place next door. The Tuesday before we opened, I was outside at midnight, painting our logo on the windows. It was the logo that Franco had drawn, and it was the first time it would appear anywhere. I knew that if I didn't get it done, it wouldn't get done, so I stood there in the pitch-black, painting by the light of siphoned electricity. I still have the sweat suit I wore to paint that night. I can't bring myself to throw it away; it has too many memories. When I want to remind myself of how far we've come as an organization, I look at that sweat suit.

I still remember the afternoon that Franco drew the logo. Giovanna was over with Romi, and we were talking about what to call this "place" I wanted to build: GiGi's House, GiGi's Place, or what. Giovanna suggested adding the word *play,* and it was perfect! GiGi's Playhouse—it sounded happy and fun! So, at six years old, Franco wrote the name GiGi's Playhouse. Then, I asked him to draw what he thought it should look like. He drew kids holding hands, with the letter *G* on their shirts. The GiGi's logo was born, and we have been building the brand ever since. We have since taken the kids out of the logo, because we serve all ages, but Franco's original handwriting is still our brand today.

The night before the opening, we'd been at the location all day, putting on the finishing touches. Paul had left in the afternoon to take the kids home. I had stayed behind until four in the morning, cleaning and willing the paint to dry. When I finally got home, dirty and exhausted, I pulled into the garage, my eyes barely open, and I noticed a strange smell, like electrical burning. I couldn't figure out what it was, but I went into the house, tired and worn-out.

"What's the weird smell in the garage?" I asked Paul.

"What weird smell?" he asked, half-awake.

"It smells like electrical burning in the garage," I told him.

"It's probably just the new car," he said casually.

"What new car?" I asked.

"I bought a new car," Paul said, shrugging.

"You did what?" I asked.

"You didn't see the new Range Rover in the garage?" he asked, as though I was the crazy one.

"I did not!" I said, exhaustion seeping into my bones.

There was no more time to talk about it that night. I just went to bed. The next morning, with all we had to do, we didn't address it either. We just went on with what we had to do.

Later on, Paul explained that he'd left the location that afternoon and had gone and bought a car he'd been contemplating for a while.

I knew it was Paul's way of saying that he could do what he wanted without asking permission. I had been so consumed with opening GiGi's that we had completely fallen out of touch with each other. At the time, I was surprised, but I have come to understand why he did it. GiGi's had become all-consuming, and I wasn't paying attention to anyone or anything else. Buying the car was Paul's way of making a statement that "We're more than this Playhouse." He was right.

Opening Day

After two hours of fitful sleep, we got up at the crack of dawn, showered like zombies, and headed back over to the location for our grand opening. When we got there, people were already lining up to get in. I remember zipping around and trying to make sure no one was touching the walls because I was sure the paint wasn't dry yet. It was completely insane! We were not prepared, like I'd hoped we would be, but as I talked to families and met children from the area, I realized that it didn't matter if we were ready for them; they were ready for us!

I walked around that day, greeting parents and hugging kids, and I saw firsthand that all parents have dreams for their children. Every single parent wants the absolute best for their children, and they will work their butts off to make sure the kids get what they need and will most benefit from having. I realized that the point of GiGi's Playhouse—the entire reason we existed—was to help them make those dreams come true.

The day of the opening, exhausted though I was, I kept thinking about all the people who had helped us reach this place. I thought about my friends who had donated time, energy, materials, and skills to make GiGi's the amazing place I had envisioned. I thought about the serendipitous meeting I'd had with Johnny B., who had offered the location, and with my friend who had given us stage curtains and designed our website. I thought about the photographer who had taken the pictures for our calendar and helped us show our kids in a positive light. I thought about the agent who had helped us out with insurance. I even thought about the doctors who had scared me and propelled me to action out of my desire to prove them wrong and to create a positive image of Down syndrome. All of these things were miracles. Some were obvious, and some were subtle. Nevertheless, they were all part of a larger whole, and each miracle—great, small, or in between—contributed to the opening of our first GiGi's Playhouse location.

I realized that even though I had been working almost nonstop on this place for five months, I hadn't done any of this alone. And in that way, GiGi's belonged to everyone, which was exactly what I wanted. I truly wanted GiGi's to be a community place, a place where everyone could feel at home. It belonged—and still belongs—to everyone.

For the opening, we gave a key to all those who came in, symbolic of their ownership in the Playhouse. I wanted people to make GiGi's whatever they wanted it to be—a place of hope and inspiration. The sky was the limit!

That day, almost a thousand people showed up. I had never seen anything like it. All around us was a feeling of pure acceptance. There was so much energy and inspiration in the air, it was tangible. We had not created a quiet, reflective clinic; instead, we'd made a riotous, loud, brightly colored place where people could be free to be the amazing, crazy, inspiring people they were. I loved every second of it!

If I needed reminders that this wasn't all about me, I kept getting them that day. Throughout the day, we took pictures of all the families and children who came in, but we didn't get a single picture of our own family. I think it was God's way of saying, "This isn't about the Gianni family; this is something bigger." Even today, every time I have an interview or a photo session, something happens to remind me that none of this is about me. I'll get a big zit or run out of hairspray, or one of my kids will forget a homework assignment and need me to bring it to school, leaving me no time to get myself ready to be on camera.

That evening, after the whirlwind day of the opening, we went to a family wedding. Giovanna was still battling cancer, and I knew that it was important that we go to this wedding, even though we were all exhausted. Something in me knew how much it would mean to Giovanna that we spend time with her that night. As it turned out, the picture I have of us from that wedding is the last family picture we all took together. It was the last big celebration we all had. I will always be grateful for that picture—and my decision to attend the wedding, which made that precious time together possible.

The next morning, we all got up and went to church. I have no idea how we managed to drag our exhausted bodies out of bed, but I think part of me thought that I should probably thank God for His role in all of this. I felt it was the least we could do.

Our family sat in the front row, bags under our eyes. During the sermon, the priest walked over, picked GiGi up, and held her in his arms for the rest of the sermon. He hadn't planned it. I had no idea he was going to do it. Father Fred just picked her up and held her as he spoke. We go to a Catholic church, and the Catholics, for all of their good grace and open hearts, are not big on improvisation. It's a very by-the-book kind of religion. And nowhere in anyone's program for the service that Sunday did it say, "Father Fred picks up GiGi Gianni and delivers his sermon while holding her." It took everyone by surprise.

Father Fred held GiGi, and talked about life and acceptance and the importance of loving those around us. He held her, and GiGi didn't make a sound. She was quiet and curious, staring out at all of us. Because we'd been at the wedding the night before, I still had my camera in my purse, so I snapped a quick picture of GiGi and the priest. I thought about how far we'd come. I thought about the mothers who had told their children to stay away from GiGi because "she's different," and then I looked at Father Fred holding my baby, with love, at the front of the church, and talking about her as an important part of the community. If I hadn't believed in miracles before, I surely did then. I watched Father Fred hold GiGi and bounce her against his hip, and I saw that she was a teacher. She still is. She doesn't have to say a word, and she gets into people's hearts.

I looked around at the faces of the other congregants, and I saw smiles and looks of love. *Right there,* I thought. *That is acceptance. That's what we're trying to do.*

The whole thing was so moving that people approached me afterward to ask if I'd planned it. I suppose they wondered why else I would have had my camera with me. (This was before everyone's phone had a built-in camera.) I can only describe it as another miracle, manifested so that I'd have a reminder of that day. But we *hadn't* planned it. I doubt that even Father Fred knew he was going to do it. There was every chance that we'd have skipped church that morning, after the whirlwind of the opening and the family wedding. We'd certainly talked about staying home, figuring that we'd put enough good into the world over the course of forty-eight hours that surely God would forgive us for one Sunday of sleeping in. But we didn't stay home. We got up and went to church. And because we did, Father Fred picked up GiGi, and she took him and the congregation to another place as he spoke. Then, he brought us all to that place with her.

Looking back, as I said, it was a crazy twenty-four hours. Beyond that, it was a crazy year leading up to the opening of GiGi's. I still don't know how we were able to pull it off in four months! With no business plan, no investors, and no idea how to do what needed to be done, we operated on faith and love. GiGi's Playhouse is a love letter not only to GiGi but also to all the children like her and to their families who need support. We were, and are, all the same; we all can help each other. With a little love, a lot of elbow grease, and a handful of miracles, our vision of a place of achievement and acceptance became a reality. I was overwhelmed and beyond grateful. I couldn't wait to see what was next.

*All of what we've accomplished has been possible
because we've been guided by a higher power.*

C H A P T E R   5

One Child, One Diagnosis,
One Community at a Time

I guess I should have been prepared for how fast GiGi's would grow, given how busy things were, but I wasn't at all prepared. I'd kept my nose to the grindstone for so long that when I finally looked up, things had gotten bigger than I'd ever imagined. Even now, I remember that period of my life by looking back at pictures of that time. It all went by so fast, and there was so much going on, that it made it hard to live in the moment when things were happening. So, now I look through my pictures and think, *Oh, yeah, I remember when that happened.* I then I think, *Holy crap! How did we get all that done?* It's a crazy feeling.

One of the things we learned early on was just how great a need there was for the kind of service we offered—throughout the Midwest, all across the country. While we'd been focusing on the children and families in our neck of the woods outside of Chicago, people nationwide were struggling with the same challenges. Without really even knowing it, we had inspired people who wanted to open Down syndrome achievement centers all over the world.

When people inquired how they could open a Playhouse, they were always shocked to find out that every GiGi's was—and still is—completely staffed by volunteers. They just couldn't believe it. Free programs, events, and activities, and we were all run by volunteers run? How could I expect people to be able to replicate that in their communities? I needed to document everything so that I could help them, but I was too busy running the flagship Playhouse and doing what I needed to do for my own family.

It Started with One

It was early 2005. Giovanna had passed away, and we were dealing with a lot of family issues with my brother and also with my parents' health. So, without a detailed business plan and no time to write one, I finally told this passionate group from Chicago's southwest suburbs that wanted to desperately open a Playhouse that they could open and I would sit on their board to help them make it happen. Not the best plan, but how could I say no to this amazing group that wanted nothing more than to serve others and create a better world for our children? They were so passionate, and I couldn't make them wait for me to try to document what I had done. Plus, my motto has always been to ask forgiveness, not permission! How do I just tell people, "This is how you run your GiGi's Playhouse"?

I would leave their board meetings, get into my car, and cry on my hour-drive home. This was partially because I was exhausted, and partially because I was so overwhelmed by the sheer selflessness of all those amazing board and committee members sacrificing their time and lives to serve our kids. Why were they following my lead, and how was I going to keep all this up?

With a certain amount of impostor syndrome, I constantly worried that I was the wrong person to be giving advice to other parents and supporters. I worried that what had worked for me—at least so far—wouldn't work for others and that all the miracles that had fallen into place for us to open the first GiGi's wouldn't be there when others needed similar help. I should have known better. I should have remembered that miracles happen for a reason, and there's no better reason than creating a place for our kids to be leaders and champions.

I hadn't had one of my "thanks you" signs in a while, so I was afraid to expand. Without a sign, I was very apprehensive to move forward. All along, I knew a higher power was driving this mission and I was just sitting in the driver's seat. I needed to be patient, and soon I began to notice the word "pleases," instead of *please,* on things I was writing in regard to opening our second location! From "thanks you" to "pleases"—I'll take it!

And so, that is how the second GiGi's Playhouse location was opened in Fox Valley, Illinois, in 2005. It was just like our original opening to launch GiGi's. My heart was full, and I left there more inspired than ever.

More to Come

With the interest growing by leaps and bounds, I realized it was not sustainable for me to sit on every board. I didn't want to hold up the launch of any more locations. So, our board really kicked into action to find a sustainable model. They researched, talked to lawyers, and, finally, in 2008, created a licensing agreement that seemed to be the perfect solution. Within nine months, we opened three more locations. First came the opening of a Playhouse in McHenry, Illinois, operated by the aunt of a child with Down syndrome. It was very weird to not sit on the board or be a part of the day-to-day process leading up to the opening. Just showing up for the grand opening and seeing their amazing Playhouse was a true gift from God. I couldn't believe it! The place was filled with kids with Down syndrome and their families; I had never met many any of them before that day. Best of all, the entire community came out to celebrate the opening. I couldn't believe I didn't have to stay there and clean up when it was all over. This really hammered it home that this was much bigger than just my family and me. It really was about the community and the larger world.

Only a month later came GiGi's Playhouse in Chicago! It was being led by some amazing parents and business leaders. I remember one of them emailing me a week before their opening. They were at one another's throats, and they didn't think they were going to make it without killing one another. You see, just because you all sit on a board together and have the same passion does not necessarily mean you will be friends outside this circle. You may need to dig deep. Look for their gifts, and see past what drives you crazy about them. Do it for the greater good; it isn't about you. Without preaching that again—because I had said it a thousand times before—I simply said "You need to look for the miracles. They are there." I then told them that the following week, when the kids would take over their brand-new Playhouse, knowing it was built just for them, all acrimony between the people setting it up would fade. I still remember the response from my buddy Aaron. "Okay, Gianni, always the damn cheerleader!"

The day of their opening the place was *packed* and full of energy. I remember looking right at Aaron as he was excitedly helping a child put his painted handprint on the new GiGi's friendship wall. When we made eye contact, all he said was "Shut up, Gianni!" He knew I was right. All the blood, sweat, and tears were now culminating into laughter, love, and pure acceptance.

Next Stop, Iowa

The next opening was Sioux City, Iowa, which was opened by a family whose two-year-old with Down syndrome had recently been diagnosed with leukemia. Even with everything the family was going through, they still managed to open a Playhouse to serve their community. Every year for spring break, we would go to Florida. I still remember the response from my kids when I told them that, instead of Florida, we were going to Sioux City, Iowa, that year! So, off we went. We drove nine hours west, straight down Route 20, to see the first Playhouse built outside of Illinois. I could not believe what I saw when we arrived. I began to cry as soon as I walked in. I felt the same Playhouse hug that I felt at our local Playhouses. They had captured the spirit of GiGi's and brought it nine hours west. They had our mural, a donor wall, the couch for families, an amazing play area, and GiGi's branding on the windows and walls. You felt the love everywhere. It was perfect!

Each of the parents and families who approached me and asked about opening a Playhouse in their area had inspiring stories of their own powerful reasons driving them to create a space where children and families could celebrate their diagnosis and be champions in the community. And though our end goals were the same, we all took different paths to get to GiGi's. One of the things that touched me the most was how interest in opening Playhouses came from so many different areas. You would expect parents to be excited and driven— and they were. But what humbles me is the amount of interest and dedication we get from other people. This still humbles me to this day. Siblings, grandparents, teachers, and community members have all hopped on board and continued the string of GiGi's miracles. It's amazing to see the motivation of others and to watch their success in creating these warm, welcoming, and encouraging places for both our kids and the larger community.

Quad Cities

Just two years after GiGi was born and one year after the first Playhouse opened, Michelle Hornbuckle-Hughes was facing her own challenge when she gave birth to her third son, Nathan, in Iowa. The similarities between Nathan and GiGi are striking. Just as I had with GiGi, Michelle gave birth to Nathan via C-section and had no initial suspicions that he was anything other than a healthy, happy baby.

"He was the best baby," Michelle said. "He ate, he slept, he was great. But there was something in his eyes. I remember friends coming in to visit me and saying, 'What is it with his eyes? When he looks at you, it's like he's staring into your soul.'"

Even though she didn't yet know about Nathan's diagnosis, Michelle said, "I knew there was something different about him from the moment he was born."

Eventually, Nathan was diagnosed with Down syndrome, and Michelle set out to support him the best way she could. When friends and family learned of Nathan's diagnosis, they began sending Michelle news clippings and articles about GiGi and me, and the work we were doing at the Playhouse, which had just gotten off the ground.

In July of 2005, a month before Nathan's first birthday, Michelle attended a national Down syndrome conference in Chicago. "As I was walking through the exhibit hall," Michelle said, "I saw all these booths and signs, and then I saw this tiny little table with a paper sign that said 'GiGi's Playhouse.' I remembered the name and the organization from information friends and family had shared with me, so I walked over and signed up for their mailing list. They were taking names and email addresses on paper—not even on a computer. I've been getting their newsletter ever since."

At that conference, we were advertising the opening of our second location. We had nothing up on our website with instructions about opening new locations because I still felt like I had no idea what I was doing! The fact that people wanted to continue the momentum of GiGi's Playhouse and make it available to children and families in other areas came as such a surprise to me that we felt like we were always playing catch-up, meeting the demands of people who wanted to open locations elsewhere. When Michelle found us and signed up for our mailing list at the National Down Syndrome Society conference in Chicago, we were still very much getting our feet under us.

Later in 2005, after Nathan turned one, Michelle began a successful buddy walk in her area to raise money for Down syndrome treatment and research. However, in March of 2006, Nathan suffered a massive stroke. While Michelle continued to work on behalf of the walk, she did it almost entirely from Nathan's hospital room.

Sadly, on August 1, 2007, after many surgeries and hospitalizations, Nathan passed away. "It would have been so easy after Nathan died to curl up into a ball and say 'my life's over,'" Michelle reflected. "But I have two other boys who are just as important to me. And I thought about Nathan and realized that, despite all of his struggles, he always had a smile on his face. He never gave up, and if I gave up after he died, it would be disrespectful to him. Getting up and moving forward is what he would want. It's how I honor him."

As they watched other Playhouses open around the country, Michelle and the executive director of her local Down Syndrome Association chapter realized that a GiGi's Playhouse might be the perfect solution for them. In February of 2011 Michelle attended the GiGi's Playhouse Chicagoland gala. The next day, she held a meeting of local parents in her area. "I brought all the information back to them and said, 'If we do this here, will you come?' They all said, 'How soon can we open?'"

At the time, we had our model in place, but we still didn't have enough detailed documentation of our processes and procedures for opening a Playhouse location. We told people who were interested that they needed a stage for self-esteem, a couch for the families to be embraced, a sign on the building for awareness, cameras for safety, literacy rooms for learning, a place to lock up cash, and ten thousand dollars in start-up funds. The foundation for successful operations was there, but we had a lot of work to do. Of course, we've changed and grown since then, and now we have a very extensive process with multiple phases for opening a Playhouse. There's a solid, strong business model that goes with it, including operating and licensing agreements and all the tools they need to succeed. Yes, we are legit! But, when Michelle started, the guidelines were much looser.

Following those loose plans, and lots of phone calls and visits to other Playhouses, Michelle moved forward with finding a location for the Quad Cities Playhouse. On July 18, 2011, they were incorporated as GiGi's Playhouse Quad Cities, LLC, and on July 19, they signed a lease on a location. The Quad Cities Playhouse officially started their build-out on August 1, 2011—four years after Nathan's death, right to the very day.

"This place works because of our families," Michelle said. "It works because of the passion of the kids, the volunteers, and the families."

While Michelle's experience was unique, she's tried to maintain perspective when welcoming new families to the Playhouse. "I'm very guarded with my experience," she explained. "These families come in with enough fear. I can relate because I've been that parent. But unless they ask me point-blank about Nathan, I don't bring it up. They don't need one more thing on their plate. With all the parents that I've spoken with and even those who came before me, one of our biggest fears with the diagnosis is fear of the unknown. When it comes with this long list of medical conditions, it's coupled with how society is going to accept our child. I don't need to pile that on these parents. I think of how reassuring our doctor was with me, telling me he'd worry about anything that might come up with Nathan's health. I try to pass that on to as many parents as possible. That's how you enjoy your children."

Even though Michelle still exercises discretion in sharing her experience with new families that enter the Playhouse, she honors Nathan every day with the work she does to bring new programming, new families, and new opportunities to the children in her community. "GiGi's Playhouse is Nathan's legacy," Michelle said. "His face is on the sign on our building. Every day, when I unlock the door, I look into his eyes. He gives me strength to keep going because our work is far from done."

Michelle, like so many founding presidents, is like a sister to me. We go through the ups and downs with the families we serve, and we grow (and drink!) together. She is a constant inspiration to me.

Making It to New York City

Like Michelle, other people have found inspiration in expected and unexpected places. The story of the opening of our New York City Playhouse is a perfect example. One day, I heard that someone was flying in from New York City to check out our two-and-under play group at the Playhouse. Tracy Nixon had a daughter GiGi's age, and she was flying around the world, trying to find the best resources for her daughter. She came to meet us and was blown away by the diversity in our Playhouse. I was surprised at the impression we made on her because, at the time, I still didn't have an office and did most of my work sitting on cases of bottled water! Even so, Tracy was so impressed by what we were doing.

"I'm not the person who can run this day to day," she told me. "But if someone who can crosses my path, we have to bring this to New York City."

Over the years, Tracy watched other Playhouse locations open, and she began working to open a New York City location. She kept checking in with us, and, eventually, she told me, "We have to do this."

Tracy asked Jennifer Patterson to join her board, and they began the process. Tracy really wanted to open the Playhouse in the financial district, putting it in the heart of Lower Manhattan. But she kept hitting stumbling blocks. She couldn't find a building that would give her a lease for a GiGi's location.

Finally, Jennifer and her father, Richard Reilly, attended the GiGi's Annual National Conference in Chicago, in November. Jennifer, overwhelmed by everything that needed to be done before they could open, said, "Dad, I think we need your help." Together, they decided that if the city wouldn't have them, they'd go to a neighborhood where they were actually needed. They settled on a location in Harlem.

Richard Reilly did not raise a child with Down syndrome. Instead, he is a grandparent to seven-year-old Louis. Trained as a builder and a designer, Richard was familiar with developing creative environments. Tackling the practical needs of opening a Playhouse location, he put his head down, pushed forward, and didn't let up until the Playhouse was ready to open three months later.

"My perspective is a little bit different," Richard explained. "I come at this from the position of a grandparent." Richard has worked in the past with the United Nations and the National Down Syndrome Society and has focused primarily on the impact and experience of grandparents. "When I was younger," he explained, "people with Down syndrome were mostly institutionalized. So, it wasn't something that anyone talked about or had any particular knowledge of. There was nothing positive to be said about it." Knowing that, Richard asked sets of grandparents what their biggest concern was. "Almost to a set," he said, "they did not talk about the concerns for their grandchild, but, rather, their worries about their own children and how they would cope with being the parent of a child with Down syndrome. They were worried about their relationships with their own children."

It's a valuable perspective, and one that GiGi's has worked to consider and address. Because of people like Richard who work with grandparents and who are invaluable in spreading the message of GiGi's, we're able to reach even more people than we would have otherwise. When we started GiGi's, my primary concern was the extended family of children with Down syndrome. I knew that many of the grandparents in our families had grown up in a different time when they had not been exposed to the acceptance we had seen. But I can't reach that community the way Richard can. That's why people like Richard are so valuable.

"I'm seventy years old," Richard said, "and when I grew up, Down syndrome was a definite negative." But now, he explained, the perception has started to change. However, it still often leaves older adults–grandparents–behind. "That's why I think it's helpful for me to be able to reach them and tell them, 'Here is my own experience.' To tell them that there is beauty out there and that there is great potential, is wonderful."

Without people like Richard, a whole segment of the population wouldn't be addressed and included. But because of his involvement– and the involvement of others like him–grandparents are now an incredibly important part of the GiGi Playhouse experience. And the more people we have involved, the stronger and louder our message will be.

"I'm also big on men getting involved," Richard said. "I think men should be involved with their families and with the world of disability. Men are often in denial about the diagnosis."

He went on to say that the objective of a place like GiGi's is to create a nonjudgmental atmosphere where people can ask questions and be completely open. "When you feel comfortable," Richard explained, "you're that much more open."

I think he's right, and it's always so heartening for me to see fathers, brothers, and grandfathers involved at our GiGi's locations. Because we focus so much on the family—and don't break things down along gender lines—we try to actively encourage participation from our dads as well. And having a role model like Richard leading the way can only help our cause.

In 2013, Richard and his wife, Marilee, toured many (nine!) of the Playhouses in the Midwest in order to experience and observe the way various locations were operating. He wanted to educate himself. Richard's visits inspired so many of our volunteers because they were able to see firsthand that someone cared how well they were doing. He was leading by example and showing how men can be involved in the work of GiGi's.

Richard also spoke about the universal nature of the GiGi's message. "The more I get involved with this," he said, "the more universal I feel the whole situation is."

Hear, hear! That has always been at the forefront of my mind—acceptance for all (yup, Generation G!)—and carrying that message outside our doors is an extremely valuable thing.

Nashville, Tennessee

The message of universal acceptance has resonated with our community and has spurred people to action. Aside from parents and grandparents, we've also had others open GiGi's locations in their communities. In Nashville, Erin Smith-Boone was a teacher who, at just twenty-three years old, realized that there were very few resources for children and families of Down syndrome in her area; she wanted to help.

At the time, Erin was teaching Cole, a young boy with Down syndrome and sensory issues. Erin reached out to Cole's mother, Melissa Wenger, to see about resources for children with Down syndrome. "Erin contacted me and said, 'There aren't many resources in the area. We should do something about that.' I laughed and said, 'Yeah, sure, I've got two kids!' But she was serious." Melissa, who had recently moved to the Nashville area from Memphis, was familiar with GiGi's Playhouse from when she had lived in Chicago. "I told Erin about GiGi's, and a few hours later, she called me and said, 'Oh my gosh, we *have* to bring this to Nashville!'"

"I was nervous at first," Melissa explained. "I didn't know what I was getting myself into."

But, eventually, as seems to happen with almost every Playhouse that opens, miracles started to occur.

Having come from Memphis, where there was a great support system in place for children with Down syndrome and their families, Melissa felt a bit at sea in Nashville, where the same resources did not exist. Because of the relative lack of support, she wasn't sure how they were even going to raise money for an opening, let alone continued operation. "Honestly, we had a garage sale for our first fundraiser," Melissa explained. "We were worried about funding, so we reached out to Nancy. She told us that miracles would happen but we'd have to look for them."

I remember speaking to Melissa and telling her that she had to believe! At that point, we'd been opening GiGi's locations for ten years, and I saw miracles every single day. I'd begun to count on them as part of our operating strategy. "Just do it," I told her, "and the miracles will happen."

As it turned out, I was right. At the beginning, there were seven people working to get the GiGi's Nashville location open. Erin,

Melissa, and a team of dedicated volunteers began reaching out to everyone they could. "With just a few moms asking, 'Does anyone know anyone?' and that kind of thing, we managed to get all the furniture and carpeting donated. We had a doctor on the board with a sister who worked for Microsoft, and so we got several computers, televisions, and an Xbox donated as well! The support from the community was overwhelming."

I love hearing stories like that. If you look for the miracles, they will come. They might be right in front of your face, and you're just missing them; but if you start looking, you'll find them. But none of these amazing things would happen without people like Erin and Melissa who believed and worked hard, even when it seemed difficult or impossible.

"Nancy told us it would happen," Melissa said. "And every time I'm like, 'I'm not so sure. We have to pay the rent here'—every time we feel like we're not going to be able to do it, a miracle happens."

The Nashville location has been open for three years now and serves hundreds of families. In fact, we just moved into a larger location to serve the growing needs of the Nashville area.

The fact that a teacher and a group of moms saw that their community wasn't meeting their needs and decided to create a place that would is what GiGi's is all about.

"We have Vanderbilt University here," Melissa explained. "And they offer reading tutoring for kids with Down syndrome, which is great. But it costs twelve hundred dollars a month. Most families can't afford to do that for their children, even if they want to."

GiGi's is an alternative that's available to everyone—for free. What an incredible gift to give the community!

Melissa is also totally on board with accepting and supporting everyone. She explained that Cole, who is now thirteen and in seventh grade, attends tutoring sessions at the Playhouse and adores his tutors. "But if someone with another diagnosis wants to come in and experience what we're doing here, they're always welcome."

Melissa echoed what I'd experienced: that while there is so much negativity in the world, spending time at GiGi's will make you see things in a different way. "There's always somebody who has a connection and sees the possibilities in our kids," she explained. "I see the goodness in everyday people all the time."

Because of that goodness and that generosity of spirit, Melissa, Erin, and the rest of the team in Nashville are still going strong.

The Road Ahead

Of course, even with the growth of the Playhouse and the new programs we've instituted, our work is far from over. I believe that part of what has made us successful in the past—and what will continue to make us successful in the future—is the inspiration we draw from those around us. People like Michelle, Richard, Erin, and Melissa, who get up every day and open the doors to the Playhouse so that others can benefit and become leaders in their community, inspire us all. We also remain in constant contact with each other, which has helped us to remain close-knit and to share successes and triumphs, as well as trials and difficulties. We learn from each other and teach one another every single day.

"GiGi's National has a three-day conference every November, in Chicago," Michelle explained. "And every year, I am in awe to be surrounded by so many passionate, driven people. It's such an honor to be included among them. The networking, training, and inspiration we receive is life changing. Running a nonprofit is not easy. Looking around that auditorium at hundreds of like-minded people who want to change the world gives you the courage to continue on, to challenge yourself, and to remember you are never alone."

The GiGi's Annual Conference has grown into a dynamic event with keynote speakers, exhibitors, sponsors, entertainers, high-level round tables, integral training, and lots of inspiration and education for Playhouses and start-ups worldwide.

The GiGi's Playhouse locations across the country are more than outposts that operate independently; they're family. Over the years, we've all become extremely close. We get together when we can, and

I'm always talking to someone, day or night. People start to learn that if their phone rings at 5:00 a.m., it's probably me calling! I am also famous for my 3:00 a.m. emails.

But that kind of casual, friendly contact is important in order for GiGi's to function as well as it does. Not a single person gets involved in a nonprofit—especially one that doesn't charge a dime for its services—expecting to get rich. Our motivations are entirely different. Even so, without our community of support and the amazing volunteers and employees and parents we have in our larger GiGi's network, none of this would be possible.

"It's our fuel," Michelle explained. "We're all sharing a mission. Every little piece of the puzzle makes us stronger and better. Every different story is what makes it work."

Melissa agreed. "It's a total team effort."

They're both absolutely right. Even though we're all working toward a common goal and for a common cause, Michelle and Melissa are both right that our differences and uniqueness are what make this whole crazy mission successful. Some of the most successful entrepreneurs and business people surround themselves with people smarter than they are. I would take that a step further and say that in the case of GiGi's, we try to surround ourselves with people whose dedication and drive match our own. It's how we fuel each other. It's how we keep pushing forward.

"Grief is an interesting beast," Michelle explained. "I wonder constantly what eleven-year-old Nathan would be like. Sometimes I see someone at the Playhouse around the same age Nathan would be now, and I think, *I'll bet that's what he'd be like.* There are days when it's hard. But those are the days when you dig deep. And that's when I try to focus on all of the success stories we've had. They encourage me to get up and move forward. I don't know what Nathan would be like now, but I feel privileged to watch other children grow."

Richard is motivated not only by the love of his grandson Louis but also by the desire to support his daughter Jenny, Louis's mom. "Your children are your children," he said. "We can't be the answer for everything, but we're there, and we try to help in whatever way we can."

Just as Michelle is driven by her memory of and love for her son, Richard is motivated by his love for his daughter and his grandson, and Erin was inspired by her students; we all push each other forward.

"I'm not doing this alone," Michelle told me.

I couldn't agree more. The adage that it takes a village to raise a child could not be any truer.

"Being accountable to all these kids and their families is an honor," Michelle further said. "I look to them for guidance and want to make them proud." She laughed. "And sassy Miss GiGi! She keeps us all in check too."

That she does! GiGi has been known to text Michelle to say, "Sorry about my mom. She's crazy!"

That's a kind of closeness and reliance you don't find in big, successful Fortune 500 companies. But because we care about the people above all, those are the relationships we develop.

"Sometimes I feel like it's more a family than it is colleagues or coworkers," Michelle explained. "Nobody's doing this to fill their pockets. Our bank is that passion and feeding our souls for the greater good. And to create a beautiful world for all of these kids to grow up and be a part of."

I couldn't have said it better myself!

Today, with thirty-nine Playhouses in operation, ten more set to open soon, and more than a hundred in different phases of the GiGi's Playhouse model, we're reaching more people than ever. What's amazing to me is the impact GiGi's programming has not just on the children diagnosed with Down syndrome but on their families as well. Michelle's sons Kellen and Conner—Nathan's older brothers—are both involved in the Playhouse programming, as are her two stepchildren, neither of whom ever met Nathan.

"My stepdaughter is going to school to be a special-education teacher," Michelle said, "and my stepson has come to programs and helped at events."

If that's not the true nature of family, I don't know what is.

Melissa agrees, saying that her daughter, who is a year and a half younger than Cole, has expressed interest in wanting to be a tutor. She was only discouraged when Melissa told her she should probably wait until she's out of junior high! That's the kind of drive and passion we love to see.

I've seen it happen with our volunteers as well. Many of those in college end up changing their majors after working with us. The fact that we have a place for the younger generation to volunteer turns them into advocates.

As GiGi's continues to grow, we will undoubtedly face challenges and struggles, like any other expanding organization. We'll have growing pains and face difficulties in trying to make our dream become a reality. But as long as we have people like Michelle, Richard, Erin, Melissa, and the rest of the GiGi's leaders at the helm, we're going to be in good shape.

"Nancy's passion and drive are addicting," Michelle said.

But I think she's got it backwards. I draw my strength and inspiration from all the children and families that work to make GiGi's Playhouse the amazing place it is for so many people. Without them, I'm a crazy lady with an idea, nothing more. But by working together and learning from each other, we are changing the world—one child, one diagnosis, one community at a time.

As you know by now, I am a big believer in signs and miracles. I think all of what we've accomplished has been possible because we've been guided by a higher power. Throughout all of it—the struggles, the trials, the difficulties, and the seemingly insurmountable obstacles—we've been blessed by miracles. Looking back now, GiGi's birth and diagnosis *were* a miracle. *She* is a miracle. None of this would have been possible without her!

I've learned that miracles are not always pretty or easily seen. Sometimes you have to search for them. They may even be disguised in pain or tragedy. It is what you do with that pain that brings your miracle to the forefront. It is finding that inner strength that propels you to action. Do not think you don't have it! You are born with it. Sometimes we just have to find it.

CHAPTER 6

Rise Above

As you begin on a journey with something you hadn't planned to have, there are so many things you have to rise above. The journey isn't a linear one; sometimes you feel like you're really down. Things might even feel hopeless. But in all of that, I've learned that there are miracles, that we are called to rise above the obstacles we face so that we can experience the blessing and the miracles hidden in them. If we don't rise above the obstacles we encounter, they can overwhelm us, they can come to define us, they can make us feel we have no choice but to give up. My best advice is that when you feel things couldn't get any worse and you see no way to get through them, that is the time when you have to rise above them—and that is what it really means to overcome.

This chapter will talk about some of the things we rise above—a diagnosis, a perception, or whatever it might be.

Rising above a Diagnosis

In a lot of ways, I feel that my life has been defined by diagnosis. I've been surrounded by it, and people I love have struggled with both physical and mental health issues for years. But I know that those people—my brother, Giovanna, GiGi—have not only taught me gratitude but also made me stronger, taught me how to face adversity, and encouraged me to believe. I know that because of all of them, I was given a choice: I could either drown in all the diagnoses or rise above. I chose to rise above, which then allowed me to move forward. A diagnosis—whether pre- or postnatal—comes with a whole host of baggage and worry, as if taking home a newborn isn't enough to worry about! New mothers of children with Down syndrome are told that their children have a higher risk for leukemia, cognitive development issues, physical abnormalities, and everything else under the sun. Instead of being sent home and told to enjoy your new baby, you're sent home with a checklist. Your child, in essence, *becomes* a checklist. Can you imagine if when a typical baby was born the doctors would say, "Your baby may have ADD, may get diabetes, and could get cancer; autism is a risk too"? Of course not, but when our kids are born, we are warned of everything that has happened to any person with Down syndrome.

When we took GiGi home, I refused to look at any of that material the hospital had given us. I thought that part of my job as a new mom—especially to a child with Down syndrome—was not to validate the medical community's negativity. I worked hard to remain positive and spread the positive vibes. I knew that reading all the scary material from the doctors about things that might happen wasn't going to help me prevent any of it, so I decided there was no point in stressing myself out even more about what *might* happen. These things that might have gone wrong with GiGi would have happened regardless of whether I was prepared for them and regardless of whether I stayed up late into the night reading about all the terrible possibilities. I put my faith in the fact that I had good doctors who knew what to look for. I decided to let them worry about it. It wasn't easy to let go of the worry, but it was the best decision I could have made—for GiGi, our family, and me.

Rising above Perceptions

Perception is another one of those things we must rise above. When I refer to perception, it includes our own perceptions, as well as the perceptions of medical doctors, family members, friends, the community, and the whole world around us. I had my own prejudices to deal with. For some reason, as I said before, in my head, I still had this terrible vision of a child with Down syndrome from the 1950s. I pictured a boy with a protruding tongue and a dated haircut. I'd shake my head, willing that image to go away, but I couldn't make it happen. I had no idea where that had come from! My mother—who worked with adults with developmental issues—surely hadn't put it there. In fact, if anything, I should have had a more positive perception of people with Down syndrome, since I had been around them for a large portion of my life and had seen what wonderful, engaging, exceptional people they were! I also had that brief but indelible connection with little Joey. In other words, I had all the evidence to disprove that terrible image, but I still couldn't shake it.

There were times when it seemed to control me. My own prejudice made me do things like tell Paul that we'd have to move again because GiGi would never be able to handle stairs. I don't know why I believed that. I certainly had no evidence that would be true, but in my darker moments, I believed the worst. Eventually, I realized it was coming from a place of fear—fear of the unknown, fear of failure, fear of this new life. But I decided to make it work for me. I coached myself to stop thinking, *What won't GiGi be able to do?* Instead, I asked, *What can't she do?* It's an important distinction. It's like asking "Why not?"

with a different inflection. Once I made that decision, things started to change. I set aside the books and the pamphlets and the folder of worry that I'd been given, and I started to raise my daughter. I figured that there was no reason for me to worry about all the possible problems instead of enjoying my child. The weight of the world was already on my shoulders with all the things my family was going through; why did I want to volunteer to carry more? Having a new baby was hard enough! I then reminded myself that I trusted the doctors taking care of GiGi, and I resolved to just raise her the best I could, as I'd done with Franco and Bella before her.

About a year after GiGi was born, I was at our lake house, and I came across the books and pamphlets I'd been given after her birth. They listed all the things that could go wrong, all the issues she could have, and all the signs I should watch for. I remember thinking to myself, *Thank God that I didn't read this stuff when she was born!* It's true that GiGi didn't develop leukemia, and we got her heart problem treated early. But even so, worrying about these things would never have stopped them from happening. It wouldn't have done any of us any good. I was so thankful I had saved myself that stress and worry. I think because of that, and because I focused on raising my daughter instead of treating her like a bomb that might explode, I was able to be a better mom to GiGi when she needed me most.

Of course, when she was born, the fact that no one would make eye contact with us was confusing, and it hurt. I began to realize then that, in addition to the medical issues GiGi was likely to face—the low muscle tone, the heart problems, the difficulty with speech—she was also coming into a world that, technologically advanced though it was, was still scared and confused and cautious about her diagnosis. GiGi being GiGi, she blazed her own trail, with the rest of us following in her wake and trying to keep up! We have made strides in acceptance, education, and advocacy, but we've got a long way to go.

Over the years, there have been many times when I think back to what Paul said to me in the delivery room. "Can you imagine what better kids Bella and Franco will be because of her?" I see that every day. I see GiGi's effect on all my kids, day in and day out. I see what amazing and inspiring people they've become because of her. But it hasn't always been an easy road.

Both Franco and Bella were young when GiGi was born. Franco was four, and Bella was almost two, so there wasn't much we could tell them initially about their little sister's diagnosis. Because most of the first few months of her life were concerned with her open-heart surgery, my other children thought that our primary concerns about GiGi had to do with her heart. For a long time, Franco even thought that Down syndrome meant that we needed to fix GiGi's heart; he didn't know anything different.

As they got older, the influence of others started to creep in, and they began to understand that there was something about their sister that wasn't typical, although—and they still amaze me to this day—they would always ask me if I was sure about GiGi's diagnosis. Franco, who is twenty one now and a junior in college, still sometimes looks at his sister, whom he loves fiercely, and says, "Ma, are we absolutely *sure* she doesn't have a different kind of Down syndrome?" He can't see her any other way; she's just his little sister.

All my children amaze me, but the way in which Franco and Bella opened my eyes to the world's perception of GiGi is something for which I'll always be grateful. That's another thing they don't tell you when your baby is diagnosed with Down syndrome: what a positive influence this child will have on your other kids and the people around her. They don't tell you all the good things. They don't tell you how she will help her siblings find their voices as well.

When Franco was small, I took him on a Mommy and Franco day. We'd been spending a lot of time taking care of GiGi and shuttling her back and forth to doctor's appointments, and I wanted to make sure that Franco wasn't feeling neglected. We were riding the METRA downtown, and I got a call from one of GiGi's locations that one of the babies in our community had just died.

Franco could tell I was upset and when I got off the phone, he asked me what was wrong.

As gently as possible, I explained to him what had happened. "Does it ever scare you?" I asked him. "I mean, because of GiGi?"

He nodded slightly, not sure what to say.

"Well," I explained to him, "our kids are a little bit more fragile. We have to be careful with them and protect them from things, but if we help them, they can do everything we can do."

"When Oliver was over," Franco said, referring to his friend who had just visited the house, "he kept staring at GiGi."

"You know," I told him, "it's just because Oliver doesn't understand. Should we show him?"

Franco nodded and smiled.

With the help of his awesome teacher, Franco and I spoke to his class about Down syndrome and what it means. We explained to his classmates that some kids with the diagnosis have low muscle tone and that the tongue is a muscle. We showed them what it's like to try to speak when you have low muscle tone by having them try to talk with a marshmallow in their mouths. We taught them how to sing "Happy Birthday" in sign language and explained that kids with Down syndrome sometimes communicate more easily that way. Explaining these things to Franco's classmates gave us an opportunity to enlighten and educate these children about GiGi and others like her.

Plus, as Paul had predicted, it made Franco a proud older brother as well. He had never been ashamed of GiGi, but now he was able to talk about her diagnosis to his friends and explain that if he helped her, she could do anything they could do. It became a cool thing for him to be proud of. He became her advocate—I think without ever really knowing he was doing it. It grew organically from his experience, and I believe that's a large reason why it's become such an important part of his life. GiGi's voice has grown strong in those who are close to her.

I decided pretty early on that I wasn't going to treat GiGi any differently than my other children. Luckily, I had a pediatrician who supported this approach. Too often, parents of children with Down syndrome are presented with a different set of measurements and milestones for their kids. There's the normal chart for typical kids—the one that looks like a rising wave—and then there's the chart for kids with Down syndrome, with different numbers along the sides.

Personally, I've never believed that anyone should be measured against a chart that determines whether so-called normalcy, so why should it matter if the person has Down syndrome? You can look at a child—or any person, really—and you can tell whether the person is healthy. The same is true for kids with Down syndrome. Numbers don't matter, and separate charts just separate us even more. It's just something else for parents to worry about.

Rising above Excuses

But even with the support of family and the best intentions, accepting your child's diagnosis is still incredibly difficult. You can say that you accept it all you want, but all the talk in the world does nothing if you don't do the work to back it up. Even when you do the work with absolute diligence and sincerity, there is a sense of self-perpetuating limits to the diagnosis. Like how I'd thought that GiGi would never be able to climb stairs. It comes from fear and prejudice, but parents sometimes rely on the warnings of their doctors and turn them into excuses for why their kids can't do certain things. I can't tell you how many parents I've met over the years who make excuses for their kids. "Oh no," they'll say, "she can't do that." Or, "He won't sit there." But the truth is, they *will* if you challenge them. Yes, it's true that some children have limitations and have to work harder on many things; stuff might not come as easily to them as it does to typical children. But there are no excuses for not doing the work because it's too hard!

As parents, we can't talk out of both sides of our mouths when it comes to the way we want our kids to be treated. If we object to having them measured using a different set of height and weight standards, we can't then decide that they shouldn't also be striving for the same milestones as typical children. It's true that sometimes things take longer, but falling back on the diagnosis as an excuse for why things can't or won't happen doesn't help anyone. If we want our kids to believe that they are capable of anything, we can't make excuses for them that hold them back from the simplest things. It's why we have to fight for our kids and why we have to teach them. It's why we have to push back and demand that they are treated with respect and that they're not just taught how to sweep the floor and wash the windows, instead of learning math and science and the other subjects taught to typical children.

Education Yes, Sometimes We Have to Rise above *That* Too

Kids—especially siblings—are often the easiest people to reach when it comes to acceptance. Children are inherently nonjudgmental—especially when they're young—and they're more open to differences. By far, we've had more problems with adults than with kids.

When GiGi was in preschool, I had her in Catholic school and public school. It was a long day but I knew she could handle it. One day, I was called into a meeting by the principal at the Catholic school. I arrived nervous, wondering what was going on. I worried that GiGi had been misbehaving or that other kids had been bullying her. When I showed up at the school, I found the principal, GiGi's teacher, and the school social worker all waiting to meet with me. My heart immediately started beating faster.

"Some of the parents of GiGi's classmates have a problem with their children being in the same class as GiGi," the principal told me.

I looked around, from the social worker, to the teacher, and back to the principal. "I don't understand," I said. "Is she misbehaving?"

The principal pointed to the social worker. "We've brought a social worker into the classroom to observe."

The social worker sat up straight and said, "GiGi can read three-letter words, and she doesn't need any help in the bathroom."

"I know," I said, still not understanding the problem. "I wouldn't have sent her here if I didn't think she was ready."

The teacher shook her head. "Nancy, GiGi has done nothing wrong."

I looked around, confused, before I realized what this was about.

"She hasn't done anything wrong, but she's being judged simply because she wears her diagnosis on her face."

It felt like someone had just punched me in the stomach. I sat there speechless. I knew preschool was an adjustment. I'd seen some kids in her class on school field trips, and I knew they were much wilder and far more uncontrollable than GiGi ever was. At least she has always listened when told to do something! But these parents judging her knew only what they wanted to know about Down syndrome. They believed all the negative things and didn't want any of it around their kids, as if it were contagious. And, worst of all, they'd told their children that GiGi wasn't good to be around. They were spreading that ignorance and hatred. I couldn't believe it.

While I was picking up GiGi that day, I gave all the other mothers the stink eye, wondering which ones had complained about my daughter. In the car that afternoon, I watched GiGi in the rearview mirror, singing along to her Hannah Montana CD, and I wondered about all the people who couldn't see her for the wonderful, amazing, beautiful child she was. I thought to myself, *I'm a hypocrite. I tell people that we can change the world, and I just got stabbed in the back by my own community.* I felt sick to my stomach thinking of how much further we had to go.

Still fuming and incredibly sad, I arrived at the Playhouse to find a new family waiting to meet GiGi and me. They hugged us both and began talking about how grateful they were that a place like GiGi's existed for them and their family. And I realized that, despite what those ignorant parents said, despite what doctors and medical professionals continued to say, and despite the negative perceptions of Down syndrome in textbooks, journals, and even dictionaries, we still had a job to do.

The day before, I had met with Thomas Balsamo, a photographer from the area. Well known for his portraits and philanthropy, he wanted to collaborate on a project to spread positive awareness for individuals with Down syndrome. At the time, we were just starting to expand and really didn't have our model solidified. I was leery of starting a big project, so we agreed to start small, with Thomas shooting some amazing portraits for our windows and marketing materials. What a gift! His work had just been published in a book on autism, and it was truly amazing. I know he was disappointed that we wanted to start small, but he agreed to it. (As you know by now, *small* is not normally how I do things, but we had the third, fourth, and fifth Playhouses about to open at that time.)

The next day, as a result of the incident at GiGi's preschool, I felt the need to make a statement even more so than ever. Meeting with the new family at the Playhouse the previous afternoon had brought me back to earth, grounding me and reminding me why we were doing what we were doing. I shut myself in the closet in the back of the Playhouse. We had no office, so I used the closet when I needed a moment to myself. I sat down on the cases of water I used as a chair, and I called Thomas.

"Game on, Thomas!" I said, determined as ever.

Working with the amazing Stephen Bagby, owner of an advertising agency and grandfather of a child with Down syndrome, they came up with the concept of our *i have a voice* gallery. We conceived of it as a traveling gallery made up of larger-than-life portraits of our kids. The goal was to show the beauty in our kids in a way that was undeniable. We wanted to show them as individuals with personalities and dreams and voices. We worked with the Loyola University Museum of Art to mount the first gallery. Since then, it's been traveling the country and has been one of our most effective conversation starters and advertisements.

So even though the experience at GiGi's school was heartbreaking and upsetting and unfair, I realized that it was also a miracle. (Yes, another one!) It called me to action and set me on a determined path. Had that not happened, I would not have been fired up enough to call Thomas or Stephen, and the gallery likely would not have gotten off the ground. The pain, the hurt, all had happened for a reason—one that propelled me to action.

Sadly, the need to rise above in the education sphere didn't end with preschool.

When GiGi was eleven years old and entering middle school, the school wanted to put her in a life-skills class. Life-skills class?! Her young brain was still learning! I didn't understand it. Why wouldn't they double up her reading or her math? Why wasn't the school trying to educate *all* our children, not just the typical ones? GiGi had done nothing but prove herself for the previous eight school years. She tried hard every day, and yet the school was still giving up on her. We have to advocate for our kids so that they can learn to be their own best advocates.

When I asked what the life-skills class was about, the teacher said, "They learn skills like washing windows and emptying the recycling bins." *What?! The only place GiGi is going to empty the recycling bin or wash the windows is at my house! That is not what she goes to school to learn.* My daughter was eleven years old and needed classes like math, science, and English, and she needed extra help with that, so why would we take the time to teach these so-called life skills, such as washing windows and emptying recycle bins? What did that show the other kids? Neither of her older siblings had learned these skills in school; why should GiGi be any different? It was—and still is—a fight, to be sure. Sometimes it's a fearsome one; but it's so worth winning! The thing that hurt me the most about it was that GiGi had never shown that she couldn't learn. And yet, they were still giving up on her. Luckily she still had teachers who believed in her and worked with me.

I truly believe that the sooner parents accept their children's diagnosis, the better the lives of those children will be. Just as limits can become self-fulfilling prophecies, so can success and achievement. Our children are incredibly smart and very intuitive; they know whether or not we believe in them. If we, as parents, truly accept the diagnosis, we won't put limits on our children; rather, we will continually work to help them to be better. We must never give up on our children, either in school or at home. Our goal must always be to help them become the best that they can be—and everything they each choose to be.

That said, it's a process, and it takes work and concerted effort. This might seem harsh, but I also believe that the harder parents are on their children—especially on their kids with Down syndrome—the stronger those kids are going to become. It's hard. It's absolutely a difficult thing to do because we love our children and we want the best for them. But it's also important that we realize that what's the best for our kids is not to have everything given to them and not to make things easy. They have to learn to strive and work toward things on their own. And as soon as parents accept a diagnosis and begin to truly own it, the faster these kids can start becoming all they are meant to be. But we've got to own it. If we own it as parents, it'll be easier for our kids to own it. And once they're proud of who they are and believe they can become all they choose to be, the sky's the limit!

Perception of Helplessness

GiGi has had no choice but to step up and try to keep up. This is partly because she was our youngest child, and partly because I'd decided to blaze my own path when we had her. As a result, she didn't get a whole lot of coddling from me. A lot of it has just been about practicality. I'm a mother of four running a growing nonprofit; I didn't have the time to be buckling my three-year-old into her seat! She had to learn to do it herself.

I know that raising GiGi to be accountable for herself is one of the best things I could have done for her. She has autonomy now. She makes choices. She doesn't get everything done for her—though she still tries to get me to do things for her, just like any typical fifteen-year-old would do. She pushes limits and boundaries. However, she does all of that because I haven't treated her any differently than I treat her siblings. Sometimes, like a princess, she holds her foot out and tries to get me to unbuckle her shoe for her. But, if I look at her and say, "No, Geeg. You can do it yourself," she'll sigh like any other exasperated princess and bend over to unbuckle her sassy platform wedges. I know she can do it, and *she* knows she can do it. We're on the same page.

This approach probably had a lot to do with the way GiGi's siblings treat her. Like I said, Franco became her advocate when he was young and was still learning about GiGi's diagnosis. Bella had her own similar experiences.

I remember very clearly one time when our family traveled to one of Franco's basketball tournaments. Since he was little, Franco has been a nut for basketball. It's his first love, and it's why he selected the college he chose. He used to play in weekend-long tournaments that he enjoyed but that were interminable for the rest of us.

Bella and GiGi got used to the boredom, and they started packing themselves a small bag to bring with them when they knew they were going to be spending all day in high school gyms. For whatever reason, GiGi has always had an affinity for the dictionary. She loves words, and she's always loved to read dictionaries. That day, Bella and GiGi had packed the *Children's Scholastic Dictionary* in their bag.

Flipping through the pages, Bella came upon the definition for *Down syndrome*. She read the definition and her face fell. She held the book up to me. "Is this true?" she asked, pointing to the definition.

I took the book and read the definition. It talked about the physical differences people with Down syndrome have, and the inherent judgment in those differences. Bella was so scared and hurt. I think it was the first time she realized how the rest of the world might view her sister. But, because she's always been a little firecracker, Bella decided to do something about it. Instead of getting angry, she took action. She wrote a twelve-page letter to the publisher of the dictionary, asking them to change the definition.

Here is part of what Bella wrote:

> The definition said that Down syndrome "is a genetic condition in which a person is born mentally retarded with eyes that appear to slant, a broad skull and shorter fingers than normal." At first, I thought I was reading the wrong definition, so I went to GiGi, and her eyes weren't slanted; they looked perfect to me. After I looked at her beautiful eyes, I measured her hand to mine. I am two years older than her, and

my hands are only an index fingernail bigger. When we were on our way home, me and GiGi were playing, and I saw no difference in her from me. We both laugh, cry, play, teach and much more.

The publisher did not respond, which was very unfortunate. A local magazine ran the story about it, though, and that really made Bella feel special.

The point of this story is that Bella was angry, and so she took action. But she did it in a positive way. That's the way a lot of positive change happens. Over the years, Bella became even stronger because of her connection with GiGi. Bella has stood up to people who were bullying her sister, and she's become an outspoken advocate. She loves GiGi fiercely and has changed the way a lot of people see kids with Down syndrome. I think it's been especially helpful for kids to see her out there supporting and advocating for GiGi. Kids are impressionable, and they learn things at a young age. The earlier we can teach them about Down syndrome and the people behind the diagnosis, the greater the range of acceptance and celebration we'll have.

Medical Care

In the past, pregnant mothers were often screened for Down syndrome because medical professionals frequently counseled expectant mothers to terminate those pregnancies. This still happens in many places around the world. In Iceland, news was made when the country announced its intention to eradicate Down syndrome and other countries are following. *Exterminate, eradicate*—words I expect to hear when I consider eliminating mosquitoes in the summer, but not when speaking about a population of people, a population of people who I love! With such statements and actions, the younger generation is apt to think that people with disabilities don't have a right to be here—that they are disposable. This is a learned intolerance brought on by designer babies and a relentless pursuit for perfection.

People react in different ways to this kind of news. Many people—a lot of them in the medical profession—welcome it. They truly believe that eradicating Down syndrome will solve a medical problem and be one less hurdle for families to jump over when navigating the rocky waters of fertility and child-rearing.

But there are arguments on the other side as well. Ignoring for a second that any sort of selective termination for a particular difference borders dangerously close to eugenics, the problems are not what they used to be. Nowadays, many women are electing not to even undergo the prenatal genetic testing for Down syndrome because they know they'll carry their pregnancy to term, regardless of the diagnosis. These people refuse to see babies and children with Down syndrome as disposable; instead, they see them as people—beautiful, unique, amazing people who can bring so much good to this world!

Regular people are different from medical professionals. While we often face fear and ignorance from people outside the medical profession, one of the issues faced when dealing with doctors and specialists is that they often have a difficult time seeing past the diagnosis to the person behind it. All they know is textbook Down syndrome. I understand it; I can empathize with the tendency to see it as a problem, but I have to keep telling myself that when the doctors and nurses see GiGi or someone like her, it's never because something has gone right. It's always because there's a problem. It's always because the child is sick or hurt or needs medical attention. I realize that it's probably the same with typical children, but, many doctors and nurses have kids of their own, and most likely see them on their good days as well as their bad ones. These same medical professionals don't immediately think of problems when caring for typical children. The same should be true when caring for our kids.

Here again, we simply have to rise above. We have to keep pushing forward, advocating for acceptance and understanding. Like so many things, a lot of this prejudice comes from a lack of understanding. That's why it's important to me that GiGi's doctors actually know her as a person. I want them to know what her favorite color is and what she likes to eat. I want them to think of her when they see her denim purse with the sequined *G* on it. I know that her care will only get better if they know her as a person, not a diagnosis.

We saw it ourselves with GiGi. She's only fifteen—it's not like she was born fifty, or even twenty years ago, when people knew much less about Down syndrome. Families faced a nearly insurmountable daily struggle at that time. Things aren't as hard as they used to be. But even so, when we left the hospital and brought GiGi home, I was handed that pamphlet for mothers of babies with Down syndrome. Yes, the one I keep mentioning! It was straight from the deep 1980s, with kids in terrible clothes and '80s haircuts. It clearly hadn't been updated in at least twenty-five years, and I wondered if people felt there was nothing new to learn. It's possible that the hospital hadn't gotten new pamphlets, or that the company hadn't printed new ones, but the message I took away from that was "This is the best we can do." It looked like they'd given up. I looked at the pamphlet and thought, *These are the kids who get made fun of in school. These are the kids who aren't able to accomplish things, because the world had already put them in a box. These are the kids who don't stand a chance.* I took one last look at that pamphlet and said to myself, *That's not a club I'll be joining.*

Once again, this bears repeating: When you take home a baby with Down syndrome, you are told what to look out for, what to be cautious about, what to examine, and what to worry about. What you aren't told is that you should treat your baby like any other baby. Believe me, no one has ever taken a baby home and stopped paying attention to it! I don't care if it's your first baby or your tenth; you pay attention to your baby. And I really believe that sending new parents of babies with Down syndrome home with a mile-long list of additional things to worry about does more harm than good. Yes, your child may develop leukemia. But you know what? So might your perfectly typical and otherwise-healthy child. What good does it do anyone to obsess over it and overanalyze every cough?

Just like with any other baby, you have to be careful. You can't sit a kid down on the kitchen floor with a bowl of Cheerios and go shopping for an hour, like you can with a dog, but that doesn't mean you have to treat your child as though he or she is going to break! I am thankful every day that I got most of my insane helicopter parenting out of the way when Franco was younger, because if I hadn't, who knows what GiGi might be like today. Instead of a typical fifteen-year-old who rolls her eyes at me and tries to manipulate me into letting her watch *Pretty Little Liars,* she might be too dependent on me and unable to do simple things on her own.

Family Who Mean Well

All of these things help us serve the people who need us. Because, despite what a preschool teacher might say, there are still families that desperately need what we're offering, and we still have to advocate on their behalf. Parents, siblings, and grandparents still need us to stand shoulder to shoulder with them in this quest for acceptance.

Grandparents are hard to deal with sometimes. The nature of a grandparent is to spoil their grandchildren, coddle them, and let them do all the things their parents won't let them do. But with kids with Down syndrome, it's often that much worse. Usually, the grandparents aren't the ones raising the kids day in and day out, so they are the ones with the time to read all the information and worry about what happens. This is also when kids are plagued by old stereotypes; this is what the grandparents know. And so, when it comes time for them to spend time with their grandkids, they want to coddle and protect and enable. Sometimes that can do more harm than good.

But there have been times when grandparents have been the saving grace for these kids. On several occasions, GiGi's Playhouse has been contacted by a grandparent who has come to us because the parent of the child with Down syndrome is having difficulty facing the diagnosis and hasn't taken any preemptive action. When that happens, the parents are often setting the child up to be delayed because of their own difficulty accepting the diagnosis. Sometimes the grandparents have stepped in to fill that role, to reach out, and to find the help their children and grandchildren need. One of the best things these parents and family members can do—not only for their kids but also for themselves—is to spend time around people who have dealt with this exact thing. There is strength in numbers, and a community like ours is built on support and encouragement.

I will always be 100 percent honest with people about what to expect—I find it especially rewarding to talk to the pregnant mothers who have just gotten what they've been told is a devastating diagnosis. I won't tell them that it'll be days of roses and fairies—I won't lie to people, because that doesn't help either—but I *will* tell them that it won't be as bad as they've been told. There is support here that didn't exist even fifteen years ago. I can't imagine how I would have felt if I'd known that a place like GiGi's Playhouse existed when GiGi was born!

I don't want another mother to have to receive that same awful pamphlet I received when GiGi was born. I don't ever want a mother to think, *This is the best we can do.* I don't want another family to put limitations on a child before they've even brought that baby home from the hospital. If all we do is offer these parents hope and an option, instead of a prison sentence, then what we've done is worthwhile.

Through experience, exposure, and advocacy, people are learning that Down syndrome is not a death sentence. People with Down syndrome can—and do—live long, full, vibrant lives. But the medical community is cautious, and the advice they give to parents—even in this day and age—is full of mixed signals. I think back to that pamphlet I was given, and I can still picture it in my mind's eye. I can still see the terrible 1980s hair and clothing, and I think, *We have a long way to go.*

When a pregnant mother refused to terminate her pregnancy after a prenatal diagnosis of Down syndrome, she had actually been told by her geneticist, "I don't expect my dumb dog to come out of the rain; what do you expect the child to do?" If people—actual medical professionals—are thinking like that, our work is far from over! In order to combat that negative stigma that comes with the diagnosis, we began creating our calendars as counterpoints—or antidotes—to the horrible pamphlets hospitals give parents. We want parents to be presented with positive, life-affirming images instead of negative, outdated ones. We've found that those calendars—the ones that show success, celebration, and achievement—do wonders to change people's state of mind. The perception matters; that's what we tell people. The perception and the attitude matter, but so does the work. It's not an easy road, but it is one well worth taking.

Please understand: I am not here to preach or to be a cheerleader for the pro-life movement. Everyone has a right to make his or her own decisions. But I can offer support to mothers and families dealing with this difficult situation. The bottom line is that things are easier than they used to be, and these kids can do everything typical children can do—with our help. GiGi is living proof! And GiGi's Playhouse serves as a counterpoint—a proof of concept—that centers like ours and programs like this actually work! New or pregnant mothers come to visit our centers, and they see the stark opposite of the handicapped, incapable, problematic children they've been told about. They see performers, artists, students, and, above all, achievers. The difference couldn't be greater.

A while after GiGi's birth, I found myself back at the hospital, taking her for some routine tests. I noticed when I came in that there were balloons and streamers set up, and the hospital was having a kind of patient fair. There were signs all over the place, imploring people to "Tell us how we're doing!" and "Give us your feedback!"

You know what? I thought to myself. *I'm going to do that.* I approached a table and introduced myself. I told the nurse working there that I'd had three children born in that hospital.

"How was your experience?" she asked me.

"With the first two, it was great," I said. "With the third one, you all took excellent care of me medically, but, …" I paused for a moment, and she waited for me to continue. "After she was born, she was diagnosed with Down syndrome, and everything changed." I went on to explain how the diagnosis was treated poorly and how no one would look us in the eye afterward. "I know no one meant to hurt me,"

I said. (And I truly do know that.) "But I will never forget that people couldn't look me in the eye."

The woman listened closely, genuinely hearing what I was saying. When I was done, she asked me, "Do you think you might want to come back and speak to our doctors and specialists?" I told her I would be happy to.

This is part of doing the work, I realized. Yes, there are many other things I could have been doing with my time. But talking to these medical professionals and getting them to see the people behind the diagnosis was one of the most important things I could do. Maybe if they start believing too, it'll become a self-fulfilling prophecy, and they'll start acting more positively. It all has to start somewhere.

A short while later, I brought a panel with me back to the hospital. We gave a presentation to some doctors and specialists, including neonatologists. We included a video that showed our kids at all stages. These were busy medical professionals with busy lives, but everyone stayed until the end. They asked questions. They genuinely seemed to care.

"It's just that we need to feel like people," I explained. "We need to be made to feel that our lives are not over."

And that, I think, is what we're up against. It's easy to teach children to be more accepting and supportive—they're kids, and they learn these things at a young age. And it's not hard to make siblings understand the importance of advocacy. If they're anything like my kids, they'll pick it up on their own. But the real challenge comes in educating adults, regular people, educators, and members of the medical community. We need to let them know that they have to *be* better. They have to *do* better. We don't need any more outdated pamphlets with bad haircuts and worse clothing. We don't need worst-case scenarios. We don't need so-called life-skills classes. We need support and encouragement. We need acceptance and acknowledgment. And we need it all *now.* People face adversity; we all do. But the trick is to face it head-on, and work through it. Whether it's a Down syndrome diagnosis or something else, no one has ever been helped by being told all the negative things that could happen. What helps is positive support, which inspires and encourages us. When we feel inspired and encouraged, we then have the motivation to rise above. That pays it forward; so, by helping ourselves, we in turn help others too. Instead of feeling frustrated and disappointed, we must compel the medical community—through our own example—to take action to change the perception of Down syndrome. We can do it. We *are* doing it. It's just like I've always thought. We have a choice: we can choose to drown in the difficulty, or we can choose to rise above and spread hope. Action on the part of the medical community will filter through to educators, and then to the larger community. When people believe that there's hope, they are more than willing to join in the effort to make things better. And once that ball gets rolling, there's pretty much no limit to how far the momentum can take us. Part of the message of Generation G is that global acceptance for all starts with faith in one another—supporting, encouraging, and empowering one another to do better and be better.

Why wait? The time is now. Let's rise above!

When you look for opportunities for learning and growing, instead of excuses for why something can't be done, your whole world changes.

C H A P T E R   7

No Excuses

GiGi's was founded as a place where we didn't look for excuses; we searched for solutions. So instead of saying, "My child can't do this," we try to get people to say, "How might my child learn to do this?" It makes a huge difference when you reframe your perspective that way. When you look for opportunities for learning and growing, instead of excuses for why something can't be done, your whole world changes. So does your child's.

I don't believe in putting limits on ourselves. I truly believe that the only way to operate is to always try to do the best you can and be the best you can. *I can't* doesn't work for me, and it doesn't work in my house. It's never been a viable excuse. But then again, I talk a good game. Even with the best of intentions, I can talk myself out of a workout in a heartbeat! I can find any silly reason not to do something

I know I should do. There's always something else I could be doing. But I try to remember that when it comes to the Playhouse, our kids, or their potential, I'm all in. I have to be. There is no *I can't*.

Throughout the founding, operation, and growth of GiGi's Playhouse, the one thing I have remained adamant about is that we don't charge a single penny for any of our programming. As a mother of a child with Down syndrome, I know how easy it is to find excuses for not doing something that's in the best interests of your child. Facing the diagnosis is hard; my job as head of GiGi's is to make it easier for parents. The bottom line: GiGi's isn't a place of excuses; it's a place of work, support, encouragement, empowerment, love, and acceptance.

After we founded GiGi's and the first location was up and running, I often found myself in opposition to what I came to think of as parental enablers. Look, I'm no stranger to crazy accommodating behavior when it comes to my kids! Remember my helicopter mode: I used to peel Franco's grapes and remove his hot-dog skins because I was a total nut about my kid's safety. We all do it; it's only natural. We want to protect our kids and shield them from anything that could hurt them. But when you have a child with Down syndrome, you realize that what they need from you is much more than skinned hot dogs or peeled grapes. And that's exactly why it's even more important that you push them and help them to grow. The harder we are on our kids, the stronger they will be.

When GiGi was still a baby, before GiGi's Playhouse, I was in an internet chat room, and a group of parents were talking about their kids, most of whom had been diagnosed with Down syndrome. One mother, who was raising an eight-year-old, asked, "Does anybody know where you can get the bigger diapers? I'm having a hard time finding diapers big enough for my eight-year-old son." A bunch of people, all of whom I'm sure thought they were being helpful, said, "I get mine here," and pointed her in the direction of stores or websites where she could order the diapers. But all I remember thinking was *These people are saying the wrong things.* What they should have said was "What strategies are you using to get him potty-trained?" Or,

"Have you tried taking two weeks off work to potty-train your child? I know it is hard, but it's so worth it in the end. Eight is too old to be wearing diapers unless it is absolutely necessary."

I don't mean to sound harsh; that's never my intention. I completely understand that there are kids who have issues that require them to wear diapers. The situation is not the same for everyone. However, I knew this family's situation, and I knew the child, and so I also knew that in this instance, the issues were behavioral, not physical. Instead of enabling her and allowing her to enable her child, I thought what we needed to do was empower her. I didn't want to just say, "This is what you *need* to do," because that's really never helpful. That feels condescending to the person hearing it, and it doesn't accomplish anything. I felt that we needed to support her and give her the strength to say, "You know what? I'm going to do this. I'm going to get him potty-trained, no matter what it takes."

It sounds like a lot, I know. It's hard to take time off work to properly potty-train your child. It's much easier to just continue buying bigger and bigger diapers. But in the end, that two weeks is an investment in your child's future and your own sanity. The reason you should do it is that your life will change too. When GiGi was three years old and potty-trained, her self-esteem grew because she was able to take care of herself, and she knew it. Knowing that your child can take care of him- or herself—and that he or she *wants* to—is liberating. It will absolutely change your life too. Though I recommend having a nice bottle of red on hand; you may need it; but you can do this!

I do not hang out in the chat rooms anymore, but I learned a lot from them. The story I just shared is only one example, but it so effectively illustrates what we do at GiGi's and why I started the Playhouse in the first place. I wanted the families to have more than just what the chat rooms offered. I mean, the early support was great; it just wasn't enough. I wanted to listen to what the families needed and provide them with emotional support, but I also wanted to provide *more*. So, we provide empathy and understanding, of course, but we take it to the next level by also providing encouragement and empowerment. We work with the families to give them strategies they can use to come up with solutions that work for them and their kids. To reemphasize, I'll use my example again: it is so much better to help moms and dads figure out how to potty-train their kids than to just tell them which stores sell bigger diapers!

To be honest, we face the same challenges with our typical children, but they are a bit more nuanced because typical kids teach and learn on their own when we can't or don't work with them. Think about how it works with any child. When they're little, you do things with them. You read, walk, chase butterflies, and build sand castles. They learn language, motor skills, and muscle memory. But as they get older, they stop wanting to do those things with you. Likewise, you get older too. Maybe you have less time, or you're more tired, or you don't have the same amount of energy to invest that you once did. Your typical child will figure out a way to learn and progress on his or her own, for the most part. But if you have a child with Down syndrome, he or she will still need your guidance. If you let it be okay for your children to do nothing, you'll end up with overweight, unmotivated, and unhappy kids.

But the best part is that if you encourage and work with your child, everyone benefits. I know that I can't get GiGi on a workout schedule if I'm not on one myself. Ours kids are like giant sponges, and they pay attention to everything we do. If you don't eat healthy, and you never work out, how can you expect your child to do those things? If you want your children to be healthier, you have to be healthier. Believe me, I know how hard it is to motivate someone else—but it's that much harder if you aren't motivated yourself. But if your child sees you and can tell that you're driven, he or she will want to do the same things.

Some years ago, I started taking a boot camp solely because I realized that I could. I'm not a runner; I've never been a runner. But I realized that if GiGi is on a workout schedule every day—and it's that much harder for her than it is for me—then I had absolutely no excuse for not working out hard myself. And I also realized that we need to be grateful for what we *can* do. Our kids live by example, and if they see us making excuses, that's what they're going to do. The more I work out, the more GiGi's going to work out. We motivate each other. And the best part is that in the end, everyone is going to be happier. The old parenting adage "Do as I say, not as I do" does not work here. You've got to set a good example, and then everyone's life improves.

Our kids have to keep moving and learning and doing. It *must* start on day one, and it can't stop! And it's hard; it's so, so hard. But that's where GiGi's comes in. GiGi's is a place where you can feel like you're not doing everything on your own. So, instead of making excuses, you can rely on others to help you through the difficult times. We've all been there, and sharing our experience is what makes it easier for all of us. People share on social media all the time about how much GiGi's has helped them, and continues to help. The takeaway here is that we all need to do what we have to do, and sometimes we need support to help us take that crucial first step. It takes courage to know when we need help and to ask for it. Find the support system you need! Don't make excuses—get help when you need it. But find a support system that encourages and empowers you to actually do what you have to do. That's the way to master your challenges, whatever they might be. Once you've done that—and not before—you can commit to being a source of help, support, encouragement, and empowerment to others. And that's how we create a better world, where everyone wins … especially our children. Yup, that's Generation G, in action!

Subtle Excuses

Even in therapeutic settings, there can be subtle blocks to progress. In 2015, GiGi's put a greater focus on adding more therapeutic components to our programming. We consulted with a team of experts who came in and helped us revamp our programming. I took a look at the programs and therapies we were offering and realized that we weren't doing enough. There were still just too many excuses: "It's too far to drive"; "My child won't sit still"; "I'm busy doing nothing" (just kidding … kind of!); "They don't listen"; *blah, blah, blah!* They just didn't get it. They had to make the investment in their child. I needed to find a way for them to see the value and time investment. I didn't want more excuses that only hurt their child in the long run. What I really wanted was to add more life-changing programs to what we already offered, and I also wanted the programs to be available to people who did not have a Playhouse in their area.

We need to help families build therapeutic play into their daily lives, and then growth will happen naturally. The last thing parents need is one more thing to do before they fall into bed, exhausted, every night. We can't make the therapy and learning different from the rest of our lives; we have to incorporate it into things we do every day. Parents don't need more on their already overloaded plates. That's not what GiGi's is about. We need to help, not make things more difficult. This applies to any aspect of our lives where we need to grow. Don't make excuses! Remember: find support if you need it—whatever form of support that might be—but keep moving forward every day. Sometimes it might feel like you only crawled an inch, but if you're ahead of where you were the day before, you've effectively moved a mile. We see it at GiGi's every day. If our kids can do it, we can do it too. Empower yourself to just keep on moving forward.

The group of therapeutic experts who worked on revamping our programming called me one day and said, "We're really getting stuck on these metrics. We're having a hard time coming up with milestones and figuring out how to measure progress."

Hoping to help, I told them, "Send me what you have." I wanted to see what they'd come up with and offer suggestions based on my years of experience of raising a daughter with Down syndrome, knowing that sometimes experience is just as important, if not *more* important, than clinical know-how. When I got what they'd been working on, I saw immediately that they were treating our kids like patients instead of people. They were getting way too clinical in their assessments and using language from the medical profession that stops meaning anything to parents of children with Down syndrome.

I opened the packet of information, and the first thing I read was the phrase "developmental milestones." Instantly, it was like I'd been transported back in time to when I was a scared mother of an infant with Down syndrome, and I couldn't do anything right. My heart hurt reading those words because, as any mother will tell you, they do nothing but make you feel inadequate. I don't care if your child is typical and healthy, when you read the words "developmental milestones," you start to panic, wondering how your child stacks up. It's that much worse if your kid has Down syndrome. You're immediately placed in competition with other children—the national average (whatever that means) and are made to feel as though your child is set up to fail against impossible goals. When your child has Down syndrome, you're told that he or she may be able to reach the lower part of the developmental milestones, and that that's okay; that's good enough. But that was never a good-enough benchmark for me. I was not okay with my daughter somehow being deemed "less than" because she didn't hit an arbitrary developmental milestone. And I didn't want to do that to our other parents. GiGi's is not clinical; we're not here to cause more hurt. And we're certainly not here to make you feel as though your child needs to progress along a medically prescribed list of milestones in order to be learning. I knew we needed to change the wording.

"We need to call it something else," I said. "We're going to call it 'purposeful progressions,' not 'developmental milestones.'" I figured that parents and therapists would be able to track a child's progress via *purposeful progressions,* without relying on comparison to others or unrealistic expectations. Instead, if you can look at a child and see that he or she is making purposeful progress toward a goal, that child is succeeding. It's not competitive, and it's not less than; it's progressing purposefully.

The issue, of course, is determining how we're going to track these progressions to see if our kids are learning. Balance and core strength is a difficult thing for our kids. Low muscle tone makes balance difficult, and the only way to make it better is with practice. So, our physical therapists suggested a complicated set of criteria for determining progress. I read the material. It said something like this: "Have child stand on left foot, assisted by one hand, holding a chair or table for balance. After ten seconds—" With that, I stopped paying attention. We're busy people! We don't have time to read six steps for one thing! Making more work and complicating things for parents isn't GiGi's way either. We need to make things simpler.

Instead of making parents jump through hoops to ensure that their children are getting the therapy they need, we need to make things easy and look for practical applications. Knowing that balance and developing core strength are important, I came up with the idea of a GiGi's balancing line. It's so simple! Basically, it's a reusable strip that adheres to a surface, like a window cling. The idea is that you put it anywhere—on the kitchen floor, in the bathroom, on the front walkway—and your child uses it as a visual cue to work on his or her balance. Something like that then becomes a part of your everyday life, instead of a specific task separate from it. Parents don't have extra hours in the day to work on intensive therapy, but they do have three minutes while fixing dinner to say, "Okay, time to balance on your line!" It takes almost no extra effort from parents, but the return on investment is huge. If your child balances on the line for five minutes while you're making breakfast and dinner, that's ten minutes a day, more than an hour of therapy a week. And it doesn't take any extra time at all. The beauty of it is that it becomes family time while they're doing it. You can be chopping vegetables for a salad or whipping up a marinade for dinner, and encouraging your child while he or she works on balance. That's what I mean about bringing home the lessons from GiGi's without creating extra work.

The other idea behind the balancing lines is that we give them to both our families and our donors so that our donors can better understand what our kids face on a daily basis. I like to give and get. And I like our donors to know what we're using their money for. The balancing line is a practical example of a low-cost, low-investment way in which we're dramatically changing our kids' lives. It's also a great way for people to understand the challenges our kids have. Most of us probably don't have the best balance or the strongest cores either, and nothing makes that more obvious than trying to balance on one foot while touching your toe! The balancing line can help everyone.

After creating the balancing line, I saw a story on neurology at the Cleveland Clinic. They were talking about brain health, and how important it is to be proactive and keep your brain in shape. One key piece they talked about was the importance of standing on one foot to improve balance and concentration. The core was my main benefit, but it is so much more.

But, it can also serve as a clarity break. Imagine just standing on that line and centering yourself. Take a moment to be grateful for what you have. Think about bringing balance to your own life. Center yourself, and use it as a time just to be present. Physical and emotional balance are equally important.

Just imagine your child's friends coming over and creating a game out of balancing on the line in the driveway. Suddenly, without even knowing it, your child's therapy has become a game, and everyone—not just the child with Down syndrome—is participating. How great is that?! One of the best ways we can remove the stigma from the diagnosis and the therapy needed is by moving that therapy into the realm of practical, everyday applications. What a great way to do it!

Once I realized how successful the balancing line was in adding therapy into daily life in a way that the child can own and have fun with, I talked to the speech therapist at the Playhouse about the homework she had assigned. "The thing is," I explained, "we have to make this practical. We have to make it part of what our kids are already doing." I thought for a moment and added, "What if we gave our kids a GiGi's branded toothbrush and water cup, and after they finish brushing their teeth, they have to do ten tongue tacos [an exercise meant to build up tongue strength and dexterity]? Then, inside the cup, what if there was a laminated word strip printed, and they had to work on pronouncing the words?"

The branding would give them a visual cue and a reminder to brush their teeth and practice their tongue tacos. They'd be looking in a mirror, and it'd be fun. The way the words would be put together would be a workout for their tongue. I realized that if each thing took five minutes—ten minutes a day if done in the morning and the evening—that little bit of extra therapy would add up to a few hours a week. And it was part of what the kids were already doing. It's so much less daunting when parents realize they don't have to find an extra two hours a week for their kids' therapy.

At our house, GiGi likes to perform on her balancing line when she's finished eating her dinner. So, we let her. What's an extra five minutes of sitting at the dinner table and watching her balance on one leg and then the other? It costs barely anything in terms of time commitment, and it does wonders for her balance and core; plus, she has an audience, everyone's happy, and it gives us extra family time. It's five more minutes to laugh, five more minutes that we're present together in that moment, and GiGi loves every minute of it.

So much of this is hard, but what I've come to realize is that it doesn't *all* have to be so difficult. There are ways to make these kinds of things easy. Everything is a stumbling block when you're dealing with a difficult diagnosis, but by giving parents and families a tool kit, we make it that much easier for them to move forward and not rely on excuses.

This extends far beyond Down syndrome. There are many different disabilities and nondisabilities alike that could benefit from thinking this way. It's just like any other change you want to make in your life; you've got to make it purposeful and incorporate it into what you're already doing. Think about diets. How often are crash diets or exercise fads successful? When people go from zero to sixty, they inevitably fall short because you cannot change everything about your life at once and expect it to stick. It's the same for therapy. It's got to be a gradual part of your life. If you do that, changes are made, and it works!

That's what GiGi's is about. It's about making it easier for parents and children to work on therapy and toward their own purposeful progressions. It's not about comparing our kids to anyone else or making parents feel badly about their children's progress. But, most of all, GiGi's is not about excuses! So, wherever you are in your own life that makes you feel stuck, no more excuses! Our kids rise above and move forward, and you can too. We empower them, and that helps them develop self-empowerment. We have to do the same for ourselves. Don't wait, and don't give yourself a million reasons why you *can't* do it. (*Ahem*—those are excuses!) The time is *now.*

If you build it, they will come.

CHAPTER 8

The Third Place

One of the best things about GiGi's is that it is a source of inspiration and encouragement, and I hope it will be that for you too. I hope it will make you see that it is possible to get through things that are hard—by rising above, by not making excuses, and by finding a support system that helps, encourages, empowers, and nurtures. That will then help you believe in yourself and others. And that is what leads to our being there for each other, in ways both large and small. When I think of GiGi's Playhouse, I'm reminded of the theme song from the TV show *Friends*. You know the one. It goes, "I'll be there for you!" (And now that song will be stuck in your head for the rest of the day because it's stuck in mine. You're welcome!)

There's a lot that's important about GiGi's. There's the support we provide for families and children with Down syndrome, the community involvement we encourage, and the demystification of the diagnosis we offer. But maybe the most important thing we give people is a place to go and a place to be. GiGi's is a place where families and children can go and be themselves. It's a place for learning. Families and children can celebrate their uniqueness and be surrounded by people who understand exactly what they're going through. It's also a place for volunteers to have a place to learn and to grow. GiGi's is just as important for the community as it is for our kids. All this makes me think of Richard, a man who is special to GiGi's and to me.

Richard Reilly, the grandfather of seven-year-old Louis from our New York City location, is one of our biggest advocates. I talked about Richard in chapter 5. He is so supportive of the work we're doing at GiGi's and the positive impact it's had on his grandson that he started the Grandparent Connection, a way for grandparents to come together and share their concerns and triumphs with Down syndrome and how it has affected their lives, the lives of their children, and the lives of their grandchildren. In Richard's words, "GiGi's Playhouse is a place where you have permission to celebrate." I think that's such an excellent summary of what GiGi's is because, as I have experienced myself, when you have a child with Down syndrome, you are often treated as though you should be pitied, not celebrated. I know our GiGi's parents feel the same way. And we wanted to give them a place to come and celebrate their beautiful children.

Remember: Richard also spent more than forty years as a designer and builder, so he knows about the importance of place in both the physical and emotional sense. Without even knowing it, when we created GiGi's, we were creating what those in community building refer to as "the third place." It's a common concept that many of us are familiar with, even if we aren't consciously aware of it. The third place is a place that is neither work nor home, but where we each can feel comfortable to be ourselves. It's where we are surrounded by friends and regulars, and where we go to feel at ease. It may be the barbershop, the local pub, or the nail salon. It's the reason why places like the Elks Lodge, the Moose Lodge, or the American Legion exist. Over the years, these places have developed criteria, including that they be free or inexpensive, are highly accessible, involve regulars, and are welcoming and comfortable. Now, I don't know about you, but that sounds like GiGi's Playhouse to me!

Just like our so-called business plan, we hadn't set out to create a place that would meet any specific community building criteria, but, because we listened to our hearts and our families and paid attention to what they needed, that's exactly what we ended up doing! And while the actual, physical buildings that house GiGi's locations are important, the people who become part of our community bring the place of GiGi's into the larger world. They make GiGi's bigger and extend it beyond the physical boundaries. The place itself allows parents, children, and families to become ambassadors for GiGi's as they bring our message into the wider world.

Richard told a story about the opening of the New York City Playhouse in Harlem, in 2012. "We'd done an open house for four weekends in a row," he explained. "We were opening but hadn't really opened all the way yet. But, one day, I was down at the location, in my work clothes, mopping the floor. We had a temporary office set up in the back, with folding tables, and we'd just received the couch a few days before. The stage was set up, and there were some things on the wall, but we were still very temporary and a long way from being complete.

"But there I was, mopping the floor, when I heard a knock on the door. I opened the door halfway, since we weren't really ready for visitors yet, and this little girl—nine years old at the time—with beads in her hair, raced in under my arm, and started slipping and sliding all over the floor! She made herself right at home! Her mother stood outside the door, peering in. 'I heard about this place from a friend in Queens,' she said. I could see that she and her daughter had taken an Access-A-Ride van the forty-five minutes to an hour from Queens to come to GiGi's in Harlem. She looked at me, confused, and asked, 'What is this place?' I opened the door the rest of the way, dropped my mop, and opened my arms to give her a big hug. 'Mama,' I said to her, 'welcome to GiGi's Playhouse.'

"Three or four months down the road, when GiGi's was up and

running and busy all the time, she came to me and said, 'Richard, that moment pretty much changed our lives.'"

I love that story! It has nothing to do with me or with GiGi. It was all Richard taking it upon himself to make GiGi's Playhouse the welcoming, comfortable, inviting "third place" it's become.

We all need people to help, support, encourage, and inspire us—and we need to do the same for others. Richard's story happened at GiGi's and because of GiGi's, but it's about so much more than that. It's about everything I've been saying since the start of this book. Every obstacle is simply a challenge, an opportunity in disguise. Rise above, stop making excuses, and do what you can every day to model the kind of caring and acceptance that will make the world a better place for us and our kids.

The great thing about the spread of GiGi's Playhouses is that every person who opens one seems to inherently understand the importance of place. And each location is unique. They all reflect the personalities of the people who are part of our community. I think that's a really important part of having a successful organization and a successful place. The New York City location isn't going to look the same as the location in Sioux City, Iowa. Iowa and New York City are very different places! People in each place have different needs and different resources available to them. GiGi's strives to be the place where they can get what they need. No one likes to be lumped in as part of a larger group, including people with Down syndrome. All people with a Down syndrome diagnosis are not the same. There are similarities and issues, like low tone, that we work to combat, but people with Down syndrome are as varied and unique as any other people in the world. A one-size-fits-all approach to treatment and therapy isn't going to work. Likewise, urban, suburban, and rural environments are different, and each has its own unique challenges. That's why I love how the people who run local Playhouses have made the locations their own. My experience is with a location in a fairly affluent area of suburban Chicago. I don't know what the Harlem location needs. But the people who run it do, and I am thrilled to rely on them for their expertise and experience, making their GiGi's a place for the community. It also means that the people who utilize a location can feel as though it belongs to them. Yes, there are some things that each location is required to have in the GiGi's Playhouse model: learning lab, stage, family area, etc. There are guidelines that we provide when someone wants to open a new location. We have GiGi's branding guidelines and the components to make a successful playhouse in the GiGi's Playhouse model. But, for the most part, people are free to put their own stamp on things and to make their GiGi's location feel like an extension of their community.

Sometimes, when I think about the growth of GiGi's, I think of the movie *Field of Dreams.* Remember how Kevin Costner's character kept hearing a voice telling him, "If you build it, they will come"? That could have been said about GiGi's! Until we founded the Playhouse and began expanding, we didn't realize exactly how strong the desire for a place like this was. But, sure enough, we built it, and people came! The bottom line is—if you believe in your dreams, you can create even more than you imagine. It really is that simple.

As we continue to expand, we're finding that there's still a need to be met. GiGi's presence in Mexico has grown, but I realize that we can't assume anything in terms of treatment and therapy available for individuals and families with Down syndrome. People are taking buses for two and a half hours to get to the Mexico location; there's much more to do. Melena, the founder of our Playhouse location in Mexico, has spoken directly to the need for a place like GiGi's where she lives. "We are still hiding in houses!" she said, referring to the lack of places for people to go for community and therapy. Years before, I was at a conference and I learned that the life expectancy for a child with Down syndrome in Mexico was fifteen years. Years later, I found that the statistic was twenty-one. There are higher incidences of Down syndrome in Mexico because people do not terminate pregnancies, but the sad fact is that most of our kids end up on the streets. The choice between the streets or hiding in houses in not acceptable. They needed a place, and now we have a location that serves hundreds of families. They do nine hundred program sessions a month and are growing at a rate of 35 percent. *Yes*—if you build it they will come!

Sometimes I think those of us who have been working with a GiGi's location for a while—particularly one like our Hoffman Estates location that's been open for fourteen years at this point—take for granted the fact that a place like GiGi's exists for us. So, it's important to continually be working with people and communities who desperately need a place like GiGi's. That way, no one has to be hiding in houses—and we all appreciate having a place to go to so that hiding is *never again* the only option for our kids.

The thing about a GiGi's location is that it's many things at the same time. It's a place for therapy—for both the children with the diagnosis and their family members. Sometimes, even if they don't share, parents find comfort in being surrounded by people who instinctively know what they're going through. It's difficult to feel alone when dealing with your child's diagnosis, particularly when there is still stigma attached to it. But being in a room full of people who understand—without you even having to say a word—is a tremendous support for people. We're a place of collective wisdom where you can feel comfortable asking your questions, knowing that someone will either have the answer or will help you find it.

People—particularly family members—also use GiGi's as a place where they can have a moment of quiet contemplation without having to be alone. It sounds counterintuitive, because the quiet moments at GiGi's are rare, with all the excitement and performing constantly going on; but, even in the midst of all that, people do find moments for quiet reflection. The best part is that in a GiGi's location, you are never alone. There is always something happening to give you hope. There is a communal need and understanding that a place for thought and contemplation is necessary, and GiGi's provides that.

But, perhaps, above all, GiGi's is a place of celebration, accomplishment, and achievement. The things people achieve with the help of GiGi's still amaze me every day. Remember that nine-year-old girl who burst into the GiGi's location in Harlem, where Richard was mopping that day? GiGi's became like a second home to her. She gets excited every time they get near the location, but she's calmed down overall. She does beautiful things every day.

All of these things comprise the reasons why I was so dead set against relegating our space to a church basement, an out-of-the-way free room, or somewhere that was difficult to find. Just as the physical place matters, so does the message the place sends. And hiding our kids and our families away from the center of the community sends the message that that's where they belong. Nothing could be further from the truth! A GiGi's in the center of town says, "We're here! We're proud! We're part of this community! Come in; welcome!"

I think of our location in Westchester, New York, right in the center of the town of Ardsley. The GiGi's location is walkable from nearly anywhere downtown. It sits right next to a Starbucks, is surrounded by a bunch of popular restaurants, and is less than a five-minute drive from the interstate. It couldn't be more convenient. It also shares a parking lot with a veterinarian, and I can't wait to see how the animals and kids can help each other. If the GiGi's locations were relegated to the outskirts of town, things would be entirely different. We like foot traffic. We like people to walk by, see the sign, and stick their heads in, wondering what we're all about. Because while GiGi's may be a Down syndrome achievement center, it is also a place for the community. And we want the community to come in!

In New York City, Richard goes out of his way to invite and involve the community in their location. An avid gardener, Richard brings his tomato and vegetable harvest into Harlem each year and sets up a free farmers' market near the location. He puts up signs that says, "GiGi's Playhouse Thanks Our Harlem Community!" And he gives away fruits and vegetables to everyone who stops by. Talk about giving back to the community! That wouldn't be possible if people didn't see the GiGi's location each day on their way through the neighborhood.

Every day, I'm amazed that we've managed to establish ourselves geographically as much as we have. I give all the credit to the talented and dedicated people who have founded each of our subsequent GiGi's locations. They have all instinctively understood the importance of place and of establishing GiGi's as a pillar of the community. We want people to think of us when they think of a place of acceptance and achievement. And we want everyone to know that all people are welcome.

The fact of the matter is that what we're doing at GiGi's can be done anywhere. We'd love for other groups to use our locations as well—that was part of my original vision when founding GiGi's—but none of that is possible if there isn't a physical place for people to gather. I love that we've provided that. The way we've created a third place for our kids, families, and the community has worked largely because it's been organic. People felt the need, and they created a place. We built it, and they came.

As we continue to expand, I can't wait to see more and more GiGi's locations popping up all over the map. I like to think of each new location as us planting our flag and announcing to the community, "We're here! We're proud! Come and see what we're all about!" And most importantly, "Welcome! We're glad you're here!"

The growth of GiGi's Playhouse is extraordinary, but our profits are not measured in dollars—they're measured in the lives we are changing, each and every day. I know our model of free educational and therapeutic programming would not fit into any Fortune 500 CEO's business plan. But you know who wins in this plan? The kids and the world!

C H A P T E R   9

Chief Belief Officer

"Be careful what you wish for." We've all used that phrase at one time or another, right? I used it as part of the title for chapter 3 because, as I can assure you, that statement is 100 percent true. I wished for an organization that would work toward acceptance for those with Down syndrome, and, beyond that, global acceptance for all. I wished for a world in which GiGi could be a healthy, happy, accomplished leader. I wished for a change, a seismic shift in the way the world treats people who are different. I got all of those things. I just didn't know it was going to be so much work to get them! Nevertheless, the bottom line is that I got what I wished for—and so much more.

In the beginning, I thought that I'd start this organization, put together a board whose members would more or less run things, and then remain in an advisory capacity myself. I wanted to raise the money for the Playhouse and give it to families and support groups so that parents and kids would have a place where they could go to make their dreams come true. I wanted this place to be completely funded, totally paid for, so that they wouldn't have to worry about raising money or paying for the programs. I envisioned it being entirely volunteer-run (I realize now how silly that was). Though we still are 98 percent volunteer run network-wide. But, most of all, I wanted it to be a place that people and their children would have as their own, free of worry.

I wanted to be involved in it, but I didn't really want to be running the whole show. Of course, that's not how it turned out. This created a lot more than I'd initially anticipated. First of all, I had four kids to raise. Beyond that, I didn't think I was qualified to be running a nonprofit organization. That wasn't my background, and it was never something I had set out to do. What I wanted was to get GiGi's off the ground, get it up and running, and give it to the Down syndrome community, thinking that they had a bigger vision. I never set out to be the person who would drive it all, who would provide the vision and the direction and passion required to make the vision a reality, but, as you already know, that's exactly what I became.

Three years in, I faced a particularly difficult time. It seemed that the more successful we became, the more other groups treated us in a less-than-positive manner. We were all volunteers giving it our all. The families we were helping and the media covering our growth and success didn't listen to the haters, which was great. We were successful in helping everybody who came to us, and we kept getting more and more families and more and more positive media coverage. I think those are the reasons why the other groups resented us. Thankfully, the negativity didn't affect our parents or kids. But I took it personally. Everyone else was able to focus on the overwhelming positives and take the criticism with a grain of salt, but I couldn't shake it off. Looking back, I think I took it personally because I was killing myself in order to accomplish all I had to do for the Playhouse and my own family.

I've spoken before about the difficulties we had with some of the other Down syndrome nonprofits out there and their unwillingness to collaborate with us. Within that group, there were a lot of haters who kept saying that I was going to turn the tables on people and start charging for services so that we could make money. Or, they said that GiGi's wasn't an inclusive place. How ridiculous! Charging for our services and/or excluding people have *never* been part of our plan! I couldn't understand why people would say either of those things. I couldn't understand why they were trying to tear us down when all we wanted to do was encourage a message of universal acceptance for *all.* The lies and negativity blew my mind.

At a particularly difficult time, the haters and negativity had pushed me too far. I was burned out and exhausted. I just wanted to be a mom again, like I had been when Franco was born. I had always thought I'd raise my kids and volunteer and do other things; it had never been my plan to spend all my hours volunteering and dedicate my life to something outside the home. But, because of my brother's schizophrenia diagnosis, I had always known I wanted to help others. I wanted to find a way for him and others with mental illness to be accepted in this world. When GiGi was born, I shifted my focus to Down syndrome, with a global message of acceptance for all. Founding and setting up GiGi's allowed me to channel my energy into something outside my family. Now I had hit a wall, pushing back against all the negativity.

So, I met with Father Fred, the same priest who had held GiGi during his Sunday sermon the day after we opened the first Playhouse location. He's been our priest for a while, and I often turn to him when I need some guidance. You can imagine that for a "don't ask for permission; ask for forgiveness" person like me, seeking guidance and advice from someone doesn't always come naturally. But I was at my wit's end and wasn't sure what to do, so I turned to Father Fred.

I explained the situation to him and told him what I was dealing with. "I'm not sure I can do this anymore," I said. "I'm proud of what we've done, but there are so many haters out there, and I'm not sure how to deal with it. People said this would fail, and now that it hasn't, it feels like people are mad at me because it's successful." I took a deep breath, shook my head, and repeated, "I just don't think I can do this anymore."

Now, Father Fred is a kind man. He's a good listener and extremely warmhearted. He's also very compassionate. Part of the reason I went to him for counsel was that I knew he'd listen, but I also expected him to support me. I think now that in my mind, I'd already decided to stop; essentially, I just wanted his blessing. Something about a priest telling me that I was making the right decision would, I felt, clear my conscience and allow me to move on. I expected him to say something like, "You did your best, and it's important to know when to walk away."

But that's not what happened.

Father Fred looked me directly in the eye and said, "Nancy, you can't quit."

I stared at him in surprise. "I … can't?"

He shook his head. "No, you can't quit. This is a ministry. What you're doing is a ministry. And it has to continue."

Ministry? I thought. That was crazy! I worked hard and I played hard, but the concept of *ministry* was foreign to me. That wasn't what we'd set out to do, and I couldn't wrap my mind around it; I couldn't think of GiGi's that way. But to see someone I respected framing what we were doing at GiGi's as a ministry helped me to change my viewpoint. A shift in perspective was just what I needed, even if it was one that shocked me.

I sighed, deflated. The priest was telling me I had to keep going. And how do you say no to a priest?

"I can't quit?" I said, knowing what his answer would be, and then adding, "But what if it is just too much for me?"

Father Fred took a deep breath. "What you're doing, Nancy, it's … well, I've never seen anything like it. I have never seen a change like what's happening with GiGi's." He considered for a second and almost seemed to be in awe. "You can't quit; you have to keep it going."

So that was it. I'd gone to a priest for counsel, hoping that he'd tell me I'd done enough, and, instead, he encouraged me to do more. I'm certainly far from a perfect Catholic, but, as I said, I couldn't say no to a priest! So, I pushed on; I kept going. This book offers a lot of messages based on my own experiences, and I keep repeating the ones I believe are the most important. (Please bear with me on that!) One of those messages is this: when you feel like you want to quit, keep going—when things seem the worst, that is exactly when the best is about to happen.

Of course, since that moment, I've come to realize that it wasn't really Father Fred I was afraid of letting down. It was the kids and families that had adopted the Playhouse as a second home. It was the parents who felt they had support for the first time, and the children who now had a voice. But, most of all, GiGi herself was the one I was afraid of letting down. She was so young at the time, and she had no ability to tell me that she needed me to keep pushing forward. So, Father Fred said it for her. Thank God, he did.

The struggles didn't stop, of course. Just because a priest gives you his blessing, the world doesn't take a step back, let you catch your breath, and then give you space to barrel forward. The world keeps spinning. Suddenly, I was faced with a lot of issues that I'd never considered before. When a typical business grows as fast as GiGi's Playhouse did, people want to buy it. You read about bidding wars in the *Wall Street Journal* all the time as corporate giants duke it out to throw billions of dollars around to buy each other out. The difference is that with a nonprofit, things just get that much harder.

But as hard as it got, I couldn't leave. You know that line from *The Godfather*? "Just when I thought I was out, they pull me back in." It felt like that sometimes.

One night, I was at the Playhouse late, probably around 10:30 p.m. I had brought the girls in earlier while waiting for Paul to get home from work, and they'd trashed the place. They always knew that if I was doing Playhouse work, they had free rein of the Playhouse, and they'd go wild! As a result, I usually didn't get to deal with mail, financial concerns, or paperwork for the Playhouse until late at night. This particular night, I cleaned up as best I could, made sure the Playhouse wasn't a total disaster for the next day, and sat down to open the mail. I was exhausted and beat, wanting nothing more than a hot shower and a big glass of wine. But I still had work to do. It was the kind of night that made me think, *I'm not sure if I can do this anymore.*

I sorted the mail, tossed out the junk, and turned my attention to the few letters and packages that had come in. I found an envelope, turned it over, and didn't recognize the return address. Slitting the envelope open, a check fell out. I opened the enclosed card and read these words: "This is for all the babies who won't live long enough and get to come and play at GiGi's." I continued reading and learned that it was from a mother whose baby had just died. She had heard about GiGi's and had dreamed of bringing her child to us; she'd never gotten the chance. I picked up the check and saw that it was for a thousand dollars.

I sat there and cried. If I had been looking for another reason why I couldn't quit, this was it. I was struggling, yes. I was especially struggling with the feeling that I was losing my social life—the life of friends and fun and socializing that I'd loved—to spend all my time working at GiGi's, to spend all my time changing the world. I was having a difficult time finding balance in my life, and I was beginning to wonder if doing so was even possible. I could feel my old, fun life slipping away. But I looked at the letter from this mother again, and I realized I had a choice to make. I could continue this mission, or I could go back to my more carefree life of fewer responsibilities.

One of the things I'd always striven for, even while raising my kids, was to find some purpose in my life outside my home and my own family. And looking down at the letter from this mother who had only wanted a place for her child, I realized that this was my purpose. Just like that, another miracle had pulled me back in. I couldn't have found—or sought—a better one.

While these miracles were necessary to keep me, and GiGi's, going, they didn't always make things easier for us. And the growth—which was, of course, amazing and fantastic—created more and bigger problems for us. When starting something, we all tend to dream big and think of what we'd do if we had unlimited resources. When GiGi's was just starting out, we'd ask ourselves questions like "What are we going to do if we have too many volunteers? How will we schedule them all?" and "What if someone wants to donate advertising space?

How will we handle that?" At the time, we'd laugh, and I'd think, *That seems like a problem for future Nancy,* while acknowledging that these would be good problems to have. Yes, they're good problems to have, in that they mean that our message is getting out there, families are benefiting from our being part of their community, and people want to help. But you know what? They're still problems, and they still have to be dealt with.

Well, four years later, we found ourselves faced with these exact problems we'd envisioned. And once we were in the thick of it, I realized that it had popped my bubble of believing that we could be entirely volunteer-run. I thought, in my naïveté, that if we weren't charging any money for our programs, we couldn't then spend the money we did have on staff. But I soon came to realize that wasn't realistic.

Eventually, we ended up hiring a part-time literacy coordinator named Jenny. Jenny was amazing. She was one of those people who truly believed in what we were doing. And, perhaps even more importantly, she believed in miracles. Some people *get* what miracles are, and some don't. Jenny really did. Jenny was just like me, in that she thought that if something happened, it was a sign that we should move forward and keep pushing. I felt like I'd found my partner in crime, except that she was paid to be there! Jenny truly loved the Playhouse. Having her there didn't give me a lot of my life back, but it did give me peace of mind. I had a believer who, from day one, could talk to a new mom. People like Jenny are so hard to find. She was a gift from God. She helped me through the opening of ten locations and was like my sister through it all. I guess only a sister (me, that is) would hide in the dark Playhouse at night to scare her! She was such an easy target, though.

One of the most important things, logistically, that I learned by running GiGi's is the difference between a for-profit company and a nonprofit. You know what it is? Tax status! That is literally the only difference. A place like GiGi's that has multiple locations, procurement concerns, fundraising, payroll, compliance issues, and zoning requirements has to jump through the exact same hoops as a for-profit business. In our case, probably more.

Eighty percent of nonprofits get their money by charging either a fee for service or a membership fee, or they are government funded. We don't have either. Our money has to come entirely from donors. So, someone has to hustle that much harder to get our name out there. We do that with advertising and marketing. But you know what else? Our advertising and marketing cost the same amount that for-profit businesses have to pay. Yes, occasionally, we'll get an in-kind donation of signage or brochures, but, for the most part, we have to pay for all that stuff. And we don't have unlimited pockets. The money all has to come from somewhere. We have donors, not venture capitalists or angel investors. (I've always loved the term *angel investors,* because, if you ask me, the people who contribute to GiGi's are the real angels, not the people with money to burn who invest in frivolous projects or products. Our angels are *believers,* and they walk the walk!) My point here is, we work just as hard—if not harder—than a for-profit business, and we have to spend money to get the word out. It's a difficult tightrope to walk.

As a result, I've come to understand that I don't need to look for investors or donors; I need to look for other believers. Sure, there are billionaires out there who understand how hard it is to run a business, and if I sat down across a table from them in a boardroom, I could make them understand our struggles. But the difference is that I'm giving everything away for free. I need to find other believers who understand not only that it's a good business model but also that it's the only way GiGi's is going to work.

All the while, I've told myself that I'll slow down when the miracles slow down. It was always my intention—even after my moment with Father Fred—to take a step back once things were up and running, and we'd become a sustainable, reputable enterprise helping people all over the country. But since 2003, the miracles haven't stopped. Whether it's donated stage curtains finding their way into the hands of my interior designer friend, or a chance meeting with a friend who just happened to have a perfect location for us, the miracles have just happened—and they keep coming.

In 2014, I recognized the need to offer more educational and career-focused programs for our adults. Plus, with almost twenty Playhouses nationwide, we also needed more office space to properly serve them. Perkins and Will, a top architectural firm, had been helping me with growth and branding strategies for our Playhouses and agreed to design our new GiGi's National Achievement Center pro bono. The problem was, once we designed it, I could not wait to run a capital campaign to pay for it. That could take years! Instead, as with the first GiGi's location, I had to go find believers to help me take the dream to the next level. There were many obstacles and many miracles.

Our landlord said, "I have never seen a project like this in all my life. When you need something, it just shows up. So many miracles that I cannot even explain!"

I told him, "A higher power is driving this mission. I am just blessed to be sitting in the driver's seat!"

I could tell he felt blessed to be around it.

So did I. I kept seeing and feeling the blessings, and more and more, they made me truly understand what *belief* is really all about. To show you what I mean, let me tell you a little more about our Mexico location. It is really *amazing,* and talk about a story! People take buses for three hours to get to the GiGi's in Queretaro, and, in most cases, it is the *only* therapy their children will receive. As I've described, the Queretaro location does more than nine hundred free program sessions a month. We opened our Mexico Playhouse during the summer of 2014, and it was our first international location. I honestly have never known a busier time. I cannot even begin to tell you what it was like to take my family to another country, where the need was so strong, and show them that a dream can transcend borders. It was absolutely incredible—the Mexico location warrants a book all its own! When they first came to me, I thought they were a little village. Then two years into helping them make GiGi's a charitable entity in Mexico, I heard them on House Hunters International. They were definitely not the tiny village I thought they were!

The new GiGi's National Achievement Center opened in October 2014, two months after our first international launch. We made every deadline that corporate America told us was impossible, including funding! Because of some angel believers we were able to open with *no debt.* There it was—a beautiful ten-thousand-square-foot national achievement center that housed a fully equipped Playhouse, a get-fit gym, GiGi University, our national offices, and Hugs and Mugs (a career training center that doubles as a café, open to the public and run by the GiGi University graduates). GiGi U is a goal oriented program for our adults to further their career skills and reach their highest potential. The tagline for GiGi U is Confident U Healthy U Whole U. They achieve this through hard work, independence and accountability. This program is truly life changing and shows what can happen when you believe!

I am so proud of the adult programming and the lives it is changing. It was truly inspired by my mom. She ran the SPRED (religious ed for adults with developmental disabilities) group at our church. All of these adults lived in a facility nearby. One day, they had a new client join the facility, but he was nonverbal, and they did not think he would be a good fit for SPRED. He had been institutionalized his whole life and would not be able to participate. My mom told them she wanted him anyway. After much discussion, my mom was very persuasive; they let him join her group. He was not an active participant, but they took him through the program, pretty much completely because of my mom. When they came to pick him up the third time, he lifted his head, saw my mom, and put his hands together in prayer. He was getting it! My mom has always told me that you never give up on anyone, no matter what it may look like from the outside. Everyone needs and deserves love, respect, and dignity—and, boy, did she give that to people.

I still say I will slow down when the miracles stop, but they continue to come! In 2016, a complete stranger, Joe Barton from Nationwide Rail Services, gave GiGi's a fifty-five-foot GiGi's branded semitruck. Yes, it's a billboard on wheels, spreading GiGi's message of love and acceptance across the country! Now, there is a believer—and an angel—and he's someone who has no ties to Down syndrome; he just wants to help make the world a better place. The truck is plastered with our logo, pictures of our kids, and our website. It's designed to draw attention and start conversations. And we never even asked for something like this! For years, I had dreamed about billboards, trucks, and anything else that would showcase our kids and our programs. My prayers were truly answered, all thanks to an angel believer named Joe Barton. It's about more than just miracles and answered prayers, though; it truly is self-fulfilling prophecy in action.

That said, I don't want to minimize the importance of answered prayers or miracles. In fact, it's a good thing the miracles keep happening, because I constantly feel like I'm not sure I'm doing things right. Back when the first Playhouse opened, we were entirely run by volunteers. When the second Playhouse opened, I gave them twelve thousand dollars of our own money, because I truly thought that was the best thing to do. I thought I was helping, but, really, I was enabling them and setting them up to fail. I know I get on our parents and grandparents for enabling our kids because of their diagnosis, but the truth was that I was doing the same thing with the organization. I wanted to protect everyone and make sure that all involved got what they needed. I wanted to make sure that they didn't have to go through the same stumbling blocks that we had with our first location. I didn't want them to have to fight for zoning or permits, or face any of the red tape we'd had to deal with. We were so new and fragile that I didn't want them to have to hear *no,* and then be discouraged. So, I helped them in every way I could, including giving them money.

Eventually, the board told me that I couldn't keep operating that way. They told me that it was unsustainable to continue to give money to new locations that were opening, and then hope for the best. As we grew, we had to put a new system in place. We had to put guidelines behind what we were doing. We needed to get national mission support, and we needed to make sure that our branding was correct. Ultimately, we had to turn our process into a replicable model that was sustainable; otherwise, I might just as well have given the whole thing away.

As I've said, the organization began solely with volunteers, and my vision had always been to continue running it that way. But, until you're in the middle of it, you really have no way of knowing just how much work is involved. The attorney general is not going to give you a break on your filings because you're just a volunteer! You really do need a professional to do that work. You can't jeopardize your organization or your mission by risking noncompliance. It has to be someone's full-time job. Growing pains are part of every business—whether for-profit or nonprofit. But, eventually, you reach a time when you just aren't capable of doing everything yourself anymore. Combine that with the fact that I never *wanted* to do everything myself, and when we got around to opening our seventh location, I was in desperate need of help. Even though Jenny was working and was a huge help, we were still operating on a shoestring budget and needed more people than we had.

At the time, my parents were elderly, and my brother was very sick. My mother couldn't take care of him on her own, and I wanted to be able to help. We all have the best of intentions, and believe that if we work hard, we can run an organization and do the job required to take care of those things.

No matter how sincere my intentions, I couldn't do it all—and I certainly couldn't run things as a full-time volunteer without an official position. So, in 2010, I came on board as the CEO of GiGi's Playhouse. It wasn't what I wanted, and it wasn't what I planned, but in its own way, it was a miracle. Once I was working in an official capacity, I began to realize how poorly we had been running things. I was largely to blame for that because I took things on faith and didn't pay attention to the details like I should have. I saw that we weren't being good stewards and weren't honoring our donors properly in the way that we thanked them. We weren't acknowledging them enough. We had great programming and were taking care of our families, but we weren't acknowledging our donors enough. We were running GiGi's with the best of intentions, but we didn't have the best procedures and policies in place. We had islands of data everywhere, but nothing was centralized. And we couldn't help the way we wanted to if we didn't have all our information together in one place. Honestly, if I hadn't come on as CEO at that time and seen how badly we were run, I'm certain we'd be closed by now. GiGi's Playhouse would be just another in a long line of failed nonprofits, improperly managed and poorly maintained.

The timing was less than ideal for our family. Even though the kids were in school and didn't need me 24-7, our personal life had taken a hit. With Paul being an S&P trader, the repercussions of 2008 in the financial markets hit us in 2009–2010. Plus, the majority of our funding for GiGi's came from Paul and his trader friends, and with the industry losing 85 percent of its value seemingly overnight, we had to find new revenue streams—and we had to do it fast.

Before accepting the CEO position, I would lie awake at night, debating whether I should take a different job to make more money for the family now that Paul's situation was precarious, or become CEO to help the Playhouse. We'd hired someone to handle our finances who'd tried to steal from us, and I still felt so blindsided that I felt like I was losing faith in people.

But, just like every other time I'd hit a wall, something happened to make my decision just a bit easier. One of the people we'd hired had been giving out some unhelpful information. A woman called from Hawaii about wanting to start a location, and he told her that we weren't doing that at the time. True, we were being cautious and trying to manage our growth in a responsible, sustainable way, but shutting down a desperate mother was the worst thing we could have done. I had no idea that one of our people was telling people this, but when I found out, I realized that we had to do better for these families.

Without meaning to, that guy had stomped on the woman's dream. It wasn't his fault; he'd never experienced the diagnosis of a child with Down syndrome and all the questions and fear that come with it. But I had. I thought about what I would have told that woman. I would have said that although we weren't currently expanding into new locations, I would try to find a way to help her and get her involved. Parents just need hope. They need permission to believe that things are going to turn out well. And I have been in her position; I understood. I would have figured out a way to give her hope and emotional support.

The decision to come on as full-time CEO was hard on a number of levels. There was the financial reality, of course. Nonprofits are famous for not making anyone rich, and when I started as CEO of GiGi's Playhouse, in 2010, I was making less money than in 1997, when I'd quit working to raise Franco! Beyond that, there were also my doubts about whether I was truly the right person for the job. Very few of the CEO duties were in my personal skill set, and I take things way too personally to be a dispassionate, pragmatic leader who has to make difficult decisions for an organization.

But after a while, I began to realize that GiGi's is different. Sure, it runs on money and donations, but it also runs on passion and miracles. And if my being passionate and taking things personally makes me fight that much harder for our kids and our families, then that's what I have to do. I don't know how to turn my personality off. I don't know how to *not* be a fighter. I take the loss of every baby personally. Every time a parent gets turned away, I get angry. That's my problem, but it's also what gives me the passion to get others to help us. It's how I find other believers.

So, I did what I thought I was being told to do, given a sign that I needed to do. I sucked it up and got to work. I knew I needed someone who knew what to do when I set out to organize GiGi's. So, I reached out to my friend Clare Ambroz. I needed someone with a brain like hers. She was a double engineering major from Northwestern, and I needed that amazing brain of hers. Always surround yourself with people smarter than you! Clare volunteered to help me, and she came in and helped us build the infrastructure that GiGi's so desperately needed. With her analytical skills, Jenny's communication skills, and my marketing skills, we were unstoppable! After Jenny left to raise her babies, we hired Kim Hanna, mother of a child with Down syndrome and Booth School graduate, as our Chief Growth Officer, and the team was once again complete. Then, we stacked our board, brought on some good legal help, and created a sustainable, replicable model that is still being used. This is the GiGi's model that is changing the world!

It was exciting, exhausting, and fun! The business concerns of GiGi's Playhouse and all the subsequent endeavors have always been secondary for me, though. My most important title is right there in my email signature: Nancy Gianni, Chief Belief Officer and GiGi's Mom. I wear a lot of hats in this organization, but none is more important than my role as the person GiGi calls Mom. That's what I return to when I get frustrated with the business aspects of the organization or burned out on the details. I remind myself that at the end of the day, that's who I am: GiGi's mom. I still feel like an impostor calling myself the president of anything or the CEO of a ten-million-dollar business. With no formal business training and an operating strategy motivated by love, I'm often shocked that I'm the person in charge of all of this. But GiGi's mom is the one thing I've always been comfortable calling myself.

A friend of mine, who knew I felt strange referring to myself as the CEO of anything, once said to me, "You know, Nancy, I think what you really are is a CBO, a chief belief officer." I've always loved that. That's how I roll. And that's how we keep GiGi's running. (For the record, I *still* feel uncomfortable calling myself the CEO!)

Part of my ability to be the chief belief officer is that I am constantly amazed by the generosity of people. That is part of what keeps me going. My first big individual donor came to me out of the blue one day. I was at the Playhouse by myself, and I got a call from a man who wanted to come and tour the Playhouse, along with his wife. I agreed to meet them there after picking the girls up from summer camp. When I arrived and met with the couple, I began the tour, and right away, I could see that what I was saying was resonating with them. The woman kept shaking her head and nodding when I explained about certain therapies and the importance of creating a place where our kids can be leaders. We sat down on the couch, and I talked about the family area. I said that it's the first place a family comes after being blindsided by a diagnosis, and when they come in and sit on the couch and take it all in, it's the first time they feel hope. I could see tears welling up in her eyes. She understood this on a fundamental level. I could see that she believed in what we were trying to do.

As we were finishing up the tour, the man turned to me and said, "What would you do with a donation?"

"Oh," I said, "we need a printer, some more books for our literacy program—we make them all ourselves—plus some card stock and art supplies."

He looked at me for a moment and then asked, "What would you do with a bigger donation?"

"You're going to let me dream?" I asked. "In that case, we need a new couch for the reading area, a new sign for the Chicago location, and upgrades to some of our locations."

The man looked at his wife, and she nodded slightly. He turned back to me. "We'd like to make all those things happen for you," he said. "We'd like to donate a hundred thousand dollars."

I screamed. I couldn't help it; it was my honest response. A hundred thousand dollars? I was floored! When he asked what we'd do with a donation, I assumed he meant with a hundred dollars or maybe a thousand dollars. But a hundred thousand dollars was beyond my ability to comprehend.

Bella, who had been playing in the other room, came running. "Mama, are you okay?" She had heard me scream, so she was worried.

After I assured her that I was fine, I turned back to the couple. "Why would you do this?" I asked. "You don't know me. I'm just someone with this nonprofit."

"We do know you," the woman explained. "We were at your 5K, and we've been watching you. We're been paying attention for a while."

I was humbled. Someone had been paying attention to GiGi's Playhouse for a while—someone who apparently had a hundred thousand dollars to give—and we hadn't even known it. It just goes to show that everything we do is important.

"But why us?" I asked.

The woman went on to explain that they'd recently had a baby, and when she was pregnant, they'd gotten a prenatal diagnosis of Down syndrome. So, they'd started preparing themselves and doing research and looking into places where they thought their child could get the necessary help. That was how they'd found us. They'd spent some time quietly figuring out what GiGi's was all about, and they were impressed with the work we were doing. Then, when their baby was born, there was no Down syndrome. The baby was born perfectly healthy, no sign of a diagnosis. These parents who, like me, believe in miracles, decided that they had to give back. So, they wanted to help us. When they were struggling with accepting the diagnosis of their unborn child, the Playhouse was the only place where they'd found hope. They wanted to help give that hope to other people.

How could I turn away when there are people like that in the world? If I wasn't there, if the Playhouse wasn't around, who's to say what would have happened to that family or that donation? But if I stayed, and I kept things running and tried to reach as many families as I could, we could make a world of difference. They just keep sucking me back in.

Because, as much as we like to say that we're a business like any other, the truth is that things are different here. Businesses don't give everything away for free, and most businesses can't afford to focus on every single individual person who comes through the doors. We have to do all of those things. So, while finding donors, balancing budgets, fixing broken printers, and plunging toilets are all important and crucial to keep GiGi's running, above all, what we need is belief, inspiration, a sustainable plan, and a constant commitment to spread our global message of acceptance for all.

One day, I hope to truly be *just* the chief belief officer of GiGi's. I would love to hand the reins over to someone else—someone I trust—so that I can sit back for a moment and take it all in. I want to be able to spend time with our families. I can change more lives if I can get to more families. In addition to giving myself a break, I'd love to be able to elevate those around me. To lift people up and give them the spotlight for a moment. I want to empower other people to speak on behalf of the organization. Other people have important things to say as well—many are more important than I am! But the bottom line is that it's precisely because I believe so much in what we're doing—in GiGi and all the kids like her—that I need to stay where I am for the time being. But I don't want to do this alone. I want people fighting alongside me! The bigger the army we have, the bigger the changes we can make. We need more believers. We need as many people as we can find who are committed to creating and sustaining global acceptance for all—Generation G—including *you.*

*Wearing her diagnosis on her face is not going to
stop this girl from accomplishing her dreams.*

CHAPTER 10

GiGi in Charge

People have called me a champion for children and families with Down syndrome, and while that's flattering and also humbling, I'd be running around like a chicken with my head cut off if I didn't have GiGi to guide me. GiGi lives in a place I would love to be. It's called *the present.* She always knows what's going on around her, and she's able to take it all in in a way that I can only envy. She's taught me so much.

We travel a lot, both for Playhouse activities and because we're often asked to speak at events or dinners. GiGi is the one who's always on top of things. It seems like every time we're headed somewhere, she says, "Um, Mom, your purse." And she's almost always right! If I had a penny for every time I've almost left my purse in the cab, well, we wouldn't need to do any fundraising for the Playhouses!

I like to think I'm organized, but the truth is that what I call "organization" is really just distraction. I spend so much time thinking about what's next—the next person on my call list or the next event—that I'm ready to walk right out of the airport when GiGi tugs on my arm and says, "Mom, baggage claim is downstairs."

She remembers things that she's learned, and she teaches them back to me. It amazes me every day. For instance, if we're in an airport and trying to find our gate, I'll get flustered and start looking all around, confused. But GiGi's always calm. She's always telling me to "Just look up." She knows where the signs are. She learned this from her friend at our New York location, who taught GiGi how to ride the subway.

"Just look up, and the signs will tell you where to go," Britt said, teaching GiGi. GiGi, in turn, teaches it to me every time we travel. GiGi has never forgotten that she got her mother—a true suburban girl—through her first subway ride in New York City. The New York City subway system can be intimidating, even to seasoned city dwellers. But GiGi took it all in stride, strolling confidently through the subway stations and looking up at the signs. She can do that because she's not preoccupied by thinking five steps ahead. She doesn't worry about having to meet with a new group of people, or whether we're going to get to the opening in time. She just lives in the present. We can all learn a lot from her.

Beyond teaching me to live in the present, GiGi also makes me stronger. She's my daughter, so, obviously, I know her well, but paying attention to her moods and feelings has allowed me to be better in tune with my own disposition.

Ever since September 11, I've hated flying. I'm deathly afraid of hurtling through the air at hundreds of miles per hour, tens of thousands of feet above the ground. I know it's irrational. I know the statistics about airplane safety, and I know, logically, that there's no way the pilot would be flying the plane if there were an actual problem. I know about all the safety precautions we have to go through, and I know that all those responsible are doing everything in their power to keep us safe. I know that turbulence is really nothing to worry about, but none of that keeps me from white-knuckling my armrest every time I get on a plane.

I used to drive to the Playhouses whenever possible—even though I know that driving is statistically more dangerous than flying. But since we've opened up more and more locations, driving to all of them has become increasingly impractical. So, we fly. And that's where GiGi comes in.

As I sit in my airplane seat, crank the buckle tight across my lap—because you better believe I pay attention to every word the flight attendant says during the safety spiel—and say an Our Father and a Hail Mary at takeoff, I turn to look at GiGi. She's smiling, nodding her head to her iPod, and dancing in her seat to Fergie's "My Humps." It's almost impossible to be stressed out and worried with her doing that! I can't help but laugh, and, just like that, she's calmed me down and gotten me through another takeoff with a smile on my face. She gives me the strength to face my fears because I know that I have to be strong for her. I know that if I panic, she will panic. And if we're both panicking, we're really in trouble. So GiGi dances to some silly song, and I laugh. That's how she inspires me and helps me find my strength. I take my cues from her.

But I know that GiGi wrestles with her own fears, insecurities, and doubts. She tries to be strong for me, but there are times when I need to remind myself that she's just a fifteen-year-old girl, even though, at times, she seems to be so much more. Every time we fly, she sees the line for security and tells me she needs to use the bathroom. I know she's nervous—remember what I said about our kids being sponges and taking their cues from us?—but she always denies it. She claims that she has a stomachache from something she ate the night before. While she uses the bathroom, I lean against the counter and wait for her. Committed to her contention that it's just an upset stomach from something she ate, GiGi lists everything she ate the previous day. It's silly, and we both know what's going on here. But in a way, it's also a ritual we go through, and there's a certain amount of comfort in it.

Where We Are Now

Our lives have gotten increasingly busier over the past fifteen years. On a recent trip to Texas, we were gone for five days, stayed in three hotels, and attended events in four cities. GiGi maintained such an amazing sense of perspective throughout the whole thing. In fact, when we got off the plane back home in Chicago, she exclaimed, "Yee-haw!" Then, of course, she fell asleep in the cab on the way home. Just another weekend for this teenager!

As much as I hate to watch any of my kids grow up, I *am* grateful that GiGi is so independent. I remember the old days, when she was little, and I'd have to do things like line the toilet seat for her. I always hated that scarves were fashionable because they were forever flipping into the toilet! At least now she can handle that part on her own, while I wait for her at the sink, listening to her recite everything she ate the day before.

The things she learns amaze me. The way she never takes anything for granted is one of my absolute favorite things about her. Even on these predictable bathroom trips that she always needs to make before going through TSA screening at the airport, she makes me smile. If the bathroom has an automatic towel dispenser, GiGi waves her hand in front of the sensor, and when the towel is dispensed, without missing a beat, she says, "Thank you, God!" I love that! I love how thankful she is, even for the little things. It might seem silly, thanking God for an automatic towel dispenser. But why not? If we can't learn to appreciate the little things in life—if we lose that sense of wonder—how can we be expected to truly appreciate anything? I love that GiGi is so thankful and that she also sees miracles everywhere. I know I get that from her.

I get my bravery from her as well. Or, I guess I should say that I borrow it, since I don't think I'm particularly brave. But, when GiGi was eight years old, I needed dental surgery on one of my teeth. I was sitting in the dentist's chair and had been so numbed up with drugs that I couldn't feel the pain. But what was worse were the noises. I could hear the electronic whirring of the dentist's drill and the shrieking noise it made when it came into contact with my teeth. It was awful! I was lying in the chair and could feel myself start to freak out, when I told myself to think about the bravest person I knew. Guess who popped into my head? Not a military general leading troops into battle, not a tightrope walker who works without a net, not even a firefighter or police officer. Nope. I pictured my beautiful daughter GiGi. And I knew that if she were in my position, she would find a way to get through it, just like she'd overcome so many other obstacles in her life. She doesn't let things stop her. Not pain, not frustration, and not someone telling her she can't do something. She just goes ahead and finds a way. To me, that's true bravery. The strength and the grace she shows in difficult situations empower me. Everyone thinks I'm the strong one, but it's all GiGi. So, I sat there in the dentist's chair, bore down, and centered myself, thinking about how grateful I was for all I had and trying to emulate GiGi. She wasn't even there, but she got me through. I know she's my daughter, though, because just like GiGi, when my surgery was over, I wanted French fries!

A typical day for GiGi would be a crazy hectic day for almost anyone. But she takes it all in stride and lives in the moment. When she was in middle school there were days when I would drop her off at 6:30 a.m., for cheerleading practice. After practice, she'd have a full day of school; then, she'd come home and work out. Plus, she is in dance at night and loves to participate in programs like Teentastic and literacy and math tutoring at the Playhouse. A few years ago, we would have had to break up those activities and space them out over a few days, but, since then, she has built up her strength and stamina through healthy diet and exercise, and there's no stopping her now. How inspiring is that?! GiGi regularly has a day that would have even your busiest adult falling asleep in front of the television, and she gets up and does it again the next day.

As I dropped GiGi off recently, I watched her walk toward the school, and I was so proud of who she's become. She juggled her big backpack and her purse with the sequined *G*. She carried a change of clothes, her headphones, and her cell phone (so she would not miss a Snapchat); she was ready for whatever the day had in store for her. She has turned into a multitasker, just like her mama.

But the thing is, GiGi has always been in charge. Even years ago, when she was less experienced with the large crowds and all the travel, she found a way to center herself and live in the moment.

When GiGi was just nine years old, Tom Ricketts, the owner of the Chicago Cubs, asked if GiGi would speak at the Cubs' big foundation gala on Navy Pier. More than a thousand people were there, along with all the Cubs players, past and present. The gala was held in the grand ballroom, which has a high, domed ceiling, soaring rafters, and up lights everywhere. It's an intimidating room for anyone, let alone a nine-year-old girl!

GiGi looked around and took in the room, and I could tell she was going into sensory overload. A school choir was singing on stage, and from where we stood, the sound wasn't filtered at all. She was scared because she hadn't been prepared for the loud sounds. That's the thing about living in the moment; sometimes it surprises you with how loud and chaotic it can be.

I knew that GiGi was nervous about her speech, and combined with the noise and chaos, I knew a trip to the bathroom because of a "stomachache" was in our future. Sure enough, minutes later, we were headed to the bathroom. As GiGi sat in the stall, I stood outside the door and made her practice the difficult words in her speech. I knew if she had something specific to focus on, she wouldn't be distracted by the music, the noise, or all the people. So, together, we practiced saying the words phonetically. "The RICK-ETTS FAM-ily, MAC-COR-MACK Found-ATION." A woman walked in before GiGi was finished and heard us practicing. I had to laugh! The poor girl couldn't even go to the bathroom in peace. But the practice calmed her. Taking those few moments to center herself had helped. She was good to go.

A few moments later, when it came time for us to take the stage, I was introduced first and quieted the room. I knew GiGi was coming next, and I wanted her to have everyone's full attention. Because, yes, these were important people we were speaking in front of. We were honored to be there and humbled that we had been asked. But as I looked around that room at all the wealthy donors, famous athletes, and fundraisers, I realized that no one there was more important than the nine-year-old girl waiting in the wings for her chance to speak. I knew that what she had to say was important, and I knew that she would do an amazing job.

GiGi stepped on stage and stood there, in front of more than a thousand people, in this huge, ornate ballroom. I worried for a moment that she'd be too nervous to continue, but then I saw her take a deep breath and adjust her dress. I knew then that she knew why she was there. She knew that she was important too, and she knew that what she had to say needed to be heard.

She blew everyone away with her speech. I know she's my daughter, and mothers have a long history of talking up their own kids, but, honestly, there are times when I watch her and wonder where she came from. She's so much more poised and graceful than I've ever been. And she knows her purpose with utmost certainty. Watching the video, I see all the ways she kept herself in the moment. At one point, I could tell she lost her place in her speech. Instead of getting flustered and stumbling over her words, she paused, ran her hand down the front of her body to calm herself, and picked up where she'd left off. Who among us would have that kind of poise? She's amazing!

And the absolute best part is how she influences other people with her confidence. Remember that when we founded GiGi's Playhouse, I didn't wait until she was older because I didn't want her to miss out on all the amazing things we'd have to offer. I wanted her to be a leader and an example, not only for children with Down syndrome but also for everyone, everywhere. And she has embraced that responsibility like you wouldn't believe. It may have taken me a while to jump fully into the CEO role, but GiGi has been all in from the start. Along the way, when I've felt like it's all been too much, I've taken my cues from her. She has *always* believed.

She has also always known her place. A few years ago, both GiGi and I were asked to speak at a sales conference for one of our donors, Patterson Medical, a company that makes physical-therapy supplies, many of which we use with our kids. Even though the conference was in downtown Chicago, only about thirty-five miles away, it took us nearly two hours to drive in after I picked GiGi up from school. Because we were so late, we didn't have time to eat before arriving. I had told the conference organizers that, because it was a school night, we wouldn't be staying; we'd just be giving our speeches and leaving. As a result, there really wasn't anywhere for us to sit at the tables in the ballroom. GiGi did not like that. She thought she was a VIP! I was too busy writing my speech to pay much attention, but GiGi kept looking around for a place to sit.

Of course, she didn't let any of that affect her professionalism. When it was time for her to speak, she strode out to the stage, confident as can be, and delivered another amazing speech. She got two standing ovations! She completely rocked it, and, as we were walking back to the ballroom, she saw an empty chair at a table of executives and sat down. She grabbed the bread basket and asked a passing waiter for her salad, as if it were the most natural thing in the world! My daughter, at home wherever she happens to be. It may seem like she's just a kid sometimes, but she has such a sense of self-awareness—the kind that I myself struggle to achieve as an adult. She is truly, truly happy in her own skin. We should all be that way. Watching her at that executive table that night, I couldn't help but chuckle to myself. I bent down and told her gently that she was in someone else's seat. Instead of being embarrassed or trying to disappear without anyone noticing—like most kids her age would have done—GiGi stood up, started giving princess waves to the room, and smiled the whole way out! We could hear the room erupting into laughter at this sassy, larger-than-life, twelve-year-old.

I truly believe that our kids were put on this earth to teach and to love. I know we spend much of our time getting them involved in therapy or teaching them new things, but I honestly believe that we're the ones who have the most to learn. I know from personal experience that GiGi teaches me something every single day. As I've already shared, her ability to be in the moment and to truly experience the present are such gifts.

And I'm not the only one she inspires. GiGi is an inspiration to everyone she meets. I love nothing more than to see her playing with the other kids at the Playhouse because I know they look up to her. And I know that she knows it too. GiGi knows that her job is not to be separate from the world but to be part of it. She understands her responsibility, but she never takes it for granted. It may be her name on the sign outside all the Playhouses, and she may get her picture in the paper frequently, but she knows that the best thing she can do is to just be herself, and to live every day to the fullest. At the end of the day, she knows that she's here to be GiGi, and that's a pretty amazing thing.

But it has been and continues to be a difficult road. Even as we traveled to Raleigh for a recent opening, people stared at her as we walked through the airport terminal. In 2017! She's not immune to the stares and the negative comments. She might joke that people look at her because she's famous—and she'll tell you that, given half a chance—but she hears the things people say.

The fact of the matter is that, despite the strides we've made, there are still hurdles we face on a daily basis. Every day, the same neighborhood kids ride by our house and don't ask her to join them. She still gets left out of lots of things because people see her as different, as somehow other.

But GiGi has proven herself every day. She can give speeches in front of a thousand people like it's a totally normal thing, and she can be the spokesperson for this movement, but she can also be such a typical teenager that she blows me away.

On our flight to Raleigh, I pulled out the manuscript of this book and set it on my tray table.

"Let me guess," she said, "you're working on your book."

"Yup," I told her.

"Your book about me?" she asked.

"Yeah, there's a lot about you in here," I said.

She leaned back, crossed her hands behind her head, and smiled. "Ah, my favorite subject."

She's so funny! She's so sassy and sarcastic and such a typical teenager that it amazes me all the time. On a recent trip to our Nashville location, I just stared at her in awe as she pulled out her iPad and worked on refining her speech as we waited for our plane to arrive. Writing her own speeches and speaking in front of thousands of people is now part of her normal day.

So, when we walk through an airport and I see people staring at her, I tell myself that it's their loss if they don't recognize what a gift she is. If people don't want to take the time to get to know GiGi and find out what a funny, smart, engaging person she is, well, they're the ones missing out.

Sometimes we get a smile from someone that says, "Good for you." But that's not always the case. We spend a lot of time working with advocates and surrounded by people who think and believe like we do. But we don't live in a 24-7 world of acceptance. The outside world can be harsh. It probably bothers me more than it bothers GiGi. I know many parents feel that way about their children. You want to protect them from everything harmful. You don't want them to hear negative words spoken about them, and you want to shield them from stares. But it's not possible to shield them from everything, and even if it were, that's not going to help them. It's just like taking the time to potty-train your children. In the end, guiding them to learn and to take care of themselves are going to make them stronger.

GiGi is the most confident person I know. Even though she can rock a speech in front of a giant crowd like she was born to do it, her life isn't perfect. She's working harder than anyone to create this movement of acceptance for all, and she has blossomed into the leader I always hoped she would be. We're not done yet; we still have a long way to go. Nevertheless, she truly is my hero. I'm not the champion; she is. I can't think of a better source of inspiration, and I hope the GiGi stories I've shared show that more effectively than I can just tell you as her mom. It may seem overly simple to say, "If she can do it, you can do it too." But it really *is* that simple. The best and most worthwhile things almost always are. Just as GiGi inspires me every day, I hope her story inspires you every bit as much.

#GenerationG—a conscious decision to be better every day.

CHAPTER 11

Generation G—Acceptance for All

When people ask me about my dreams for the future and my hopes for GiGi's Playhouse, I have a tendency to talk about the things I know we can accomplish before really going big and admitting that we want to change the world. What we really want is global acceptance for all. At the end of the day, that's what we're trying to do here. This goes way beyond the Down syndrome community. We're talking about acceptance for absolutely everyone. I have always had a larger message of global acceptance for *all*—that is where #GenerationG comes in. That's what Generation G is: a conscious decision to be better every day. Be kind; be generous; be accepting. It's a big task, but I think we're up to it.

When we talk about global acceptance, I wonder what more we can do. Our GiGi's Playhouse locations are paid for 24-7, and because we had to work so hard to get to that point, I want them to be in use every hour of the day, by someone who needs them. Remember—although GiGi's serves those with Down syndrome and their families, first and foremost, GiGi's is for the entire community. Here again, this is Generation G—global acceptance—and so much more. Acceptance is a key step toward building the kind of community that makes each of us better, which in turn makes our world better. By making GiGi's accessible to the community, we embrace the community, offering the opportunity for them to pay it forward, embrace us, and so on. It's the same idea I've been expressing all along. Here's a story that shows it in action.

When we opened the first Playhouse, a mother who ran a cerebral palsy support group called me. They had been meeting at the library, and they asked if they could use GiGi's when we weren't using it. Nothing makes me happier than to see a GiGi's location in continual use, so I said yes right away. I told them I would try to get there myself to explain how things worked, but my son had a baseball game, and so I might not be by until later. At the time, we were still keeping a key at the bakery next door; I told them where to find it, and left a list of instructions about how to work the lights, sound system, etc.

Of course, Franco's baseball game went into extra innings, and it got late. I knew I wasn't going to make it to the Playhouse like I wanted, so I called to see how they were doing. The phone rang a few times, and, eventually, a tentative voice answered, "GiGi's Playhouse?" They didn't know if they should answer the phone after hours, but they didn't want us to miss something important.

"I'm just checking in," I explained. "Just wanted to make sure everything is going all right."

The woman paused for a moment; she seemed overwhelmed. Finally, she spoke. "Oh, Nancy," she told me. "A mom was just having a really emotional moment, and she needed our help. We're so glad we're here. If we had been at the library, the janitor would have been kicking us out right now! Thank you so much for this place."

I couldn't have been happier. All I wanted was to create a safe, welcoming, supportive place for anyone who needed it. The most important thing is that we're achieving our mission by presenting our kids as larger than life and promoting the message of acceptance for all, and if working toward that goal means loaning out our locations for autism awareness or multiple sclerosis therapy, or any type of group meetings, we're absolutely going to do it. That's why we kept the key at the bakery for ten years; anyone could use it. Now we have a keypad, so we can keep sharing the love!

I would also love more time with all the GiGi's location founders and teams. Talk about a dynamic group of people stepping up to change the world. We recently started a founders' circle. Together, we dream and collaborate about our next big adventures. It is absolutely amazing. Every location is founded by a woman (with a lot of help), so, to have us all together, empowering each other, sharing our stories, and thinking of ways to help the start-up Playhouses—and also secure funding nationally so that every location can focus more on programs and families, not fundraising—this is a dream I have had from the beginning. Now I have an amazing team to help make that happen. What I love about these women is that they did their jobs, they each opened their Playhouse, and yet they still want to do more. I would love to have a panel of GiGi's founders traveling to different venues and sharing their stories of determination against some pretty unsurmountable obstacles. It really solidifies my statement that we all have the strength to change the world; sometimes we just have to find that strength within us.

That strength is sometimes hard to find, especially as an adolescent. This is where Generation G comes in again; we need to teach it to our young people every day, and we need to model it every day—be generous, be kind, be accepting. When they see that conscious choice alive in every decision and every action on a daily basis, it becomes automatic for them. I've come to realize that the kind of acceptance I'm talking about requires a generational change, though it isn't defined by age group. That's what Generation G is about: inspiring the future generation to make that change, to fight for acceptance, and to never give up.

I also know that the fight is real, it's big, and it's still here at home.

Just the other day, I got a text from my Bella, now in high school. It read, in all caps, "GIGI'S NAME IS NOT AN INSULT!"

Worried, I wrote back and asked her what was wrong.

A short while later, she called me and explained that a classmate of hers had been making fun of someone, saying, "What are you, a Down syndrome retard? Do you belong at GiGi's Playhouse?"

Bella started fuming.

"Mom," she said, "people have been calling kids a 'GiGi,' like it's an insult."

I tried to remain calm, knowing that what I really wanted to do was fly down to that school, grab that kid by the back of the shirt, and yell at him until I turned blue in the face. I knew that wouldn't help any of us.

"What did you do?" I asked Bella.

"I took notes," she told me. "I sat down in the corner and wrote down everything I wanted to say to him. I wanted him to understand what he was doing was so wrong."

Despite the pain I was feeling for all of my kids, I was so proud of Bella. Still a teenager, and she was handling this better than her mama. She had taken stock of what had happened and prioritized what she needed to do to make the incident a learning experience. When we got off the phone, she had a well-thought-out plan for how she was going to approach the kid. She wasn't there to confront but to teach. Of course, I still wanted to kick the kid's ass, but I was so proud of her.

Later that day, she went looking for the kid who had said such insulting things. The teacher asked her what she wanted, and Bella explained.

"This is really something the dean should handle," the teacher said.

Bella, knowing that if it went to the dean, the educational opportunity would be lost, left the classroom and waited outside. Finally, the student emerged, the last one out of the classroom.

He looked right at Bella. "What do you want?" the six-foot bully asked her.

"I want to talk to you," she said calmly.

"I have to get to class," he said, pushing past her.

"Can I walk with you?" she asked, undeterred.

The boy shrugged. "I guess," he said.

They started to walk, and Bella spoke calmly, letting the boy know that he'd been hurtful. "Don't you understand that GiGi can't help it? She's my sister, and I love her. She cannot help it that she has Down syndrome. It's not nice to make fun of GiGi or people like her. And it's not nice to make fun of a place that's there to help them. My family built that place out of love."

After some more lecturing from Bella, the boy turned to face her. "What do you want from me?" he asked. "You want me to apologize?"

"Um, yeah, I think I do," Bella said.

"Fine," the boy said. "I'm sorry."

Bella considered for a moment and knew he didn't mean it, so she said, "No, that doesn't work. Don't you understand that it really hurts when you say things like that?"

I'm sure she wanted to scream, but, like a pro, she kept her composure.

Finally, the boy looked defeated, as though he realized he'd been saying terrible things. "Okay," he relented, "I really am sorry. I didn't realize it would hurt people. I will never do that again."

"Thank you," Bella said, knowing he really meant it, and turned away.

This is Generation G in action!

Back when GiGi was born, Paul and I agreed that she would make our other kids that much stronger. And, while I see it in them every day, it never ceases to amaze me how much they've grown and how amazing they've become. Bella champions her sister every single day. Bella is the epitome of Generation G. The story I shared above illustrates this more effectively than I could possibly just say. (I'm her mom, so I can't help but be biased about how awesome she is! I think you'll let me do that, right?) The point is, Bella turned what could have been an ugly confrontation into a learning experience, and she did it better than I could have. Since that incident, she's started a

Generation G club at her high school. Knowing Bella, it's only going to grow from there—the sky's the limit!

I see all of this—the struggle and achievements—in GiGi. Like her big sister, Bella, GiGi embodies Generation G in her own unique way. Every day, I see changes in GiGi that amaze me. I've come to realize that the times I've seen her grow the most are the times when she's been the most independent. She knows she's in charge of her own life, and she feels empowered to make decisions and act like the sassy young lady she is.

It started as early as three years old, when I brought her to school and she was no longer in diapers. She might have been three—and she'd probably kill me for saying this now—but she thought she was hot stuff! She knew she was independent and in control, and she acted like it.

I have seen that many times throughout her life. We travel a lot, as I've said, and she's so poised and practiced; it's like she was born for this. I can't get over what a natural she is. (I know I keep saying this, but it's true!) It started when I told her that she had to be responsible for herself. She has to know where her bags are—she often knows where mine are too! And she has to be responsible for getting herself dressed and ready and making sure she has everything she needs. All my other kids have lost or broken their phones at least once, but not GiGi. She's had hers for over two years now. When I tell her she needs to be in charge of something, she embraces that responsibility; no problem. She knows she represents the GiGi's Playhouse organization, and she takes that responsibility seriously. It's her name up there on the sign!

And yet, one of the greatest changes I've seen in her was when she decided to do something at school that she hadn't done before. When GiGi turned thirteen, she decided she wanted to be a cheerleader. At first, I was concerned. I wanted to be sure that she was physically up to the challenge, since she'd be on a team with typical kids. Using her as a mascot was not what we were looking for. So, I told her, "Geeg, if you want to do this, you're responsible. You have to work hard, go to practice, and make sure you do everything you need to do to be part of the team." She agreed, and from almost the second she became a member of that cheerleading team, I saw her grow. She became part of a new group that accepted her. And she did it all by herself. She knows she fits in, and she acts like it. She doesn't have an aide or anyone walking with her to practice and telling her what to do. She's on her own, and she's flourishing.

Franco had been away at college for about a month when he came home for Thanksgiving. It was the first time he'd seen GiGi since she'd begun cheerleading. "Mom," he told me, "I don't know if you can see it, because you're around her all the time, but I see such a difference in her."

"I see it," I told him, and we both marveled at what a strong and independent young woman GiGi had become.

It comes down to empowering our kids. They have to know that you trust them and believe in them, and then you set them free. But you also have to allow them to fail on their own, so they learn the hard lessons. It's difficult, but it's so important, both for you and your children.

When GiGi was little, she would often get away with things that she shouldn't have, because I was trying to do twenty things at once, and something slipped through the cracks. I didn't have time to hold her accountable. When she was three, she went through a phase where she became a runner, and she was forever running to the karate studio next to the Playhouse. Every time we'd drive up, she'd get out of the car and run to the karate studio. I'd have to grab her and bring her back inside. Kids learn to test their limits very early, and she knew I wasn't going to discipline her because I just had too many other things to do.

One day, I'd had enough. I knew she was perfectly capable of listening if I'd only hold her accountable for her actions. So, on our way to the Playhouse, I started talking it up. "Veronica and Jessica are going to be there," I said, getting her excited to see her friends. "It's going to be so much fun! You're going to have such a good time."

She got excited, anxious to play with her friends.

Of course, when we arrived, I opened her door, and, as usual, she made a beeline for the karate studio. But this time, instead of grabbing her, bringing her into the Playhouse, and ignoring it, I put her right back in the car. "That's it," I said. "If you can't behave, you don't get to play with your friends." I turned around and drove right back home.

GiGi didn't know that I had only planned to stop at the Playhouse for a moment and that I had no intention of staying. But she learned there were consequences to her actions, and she realized that she had to be accountable for what she did. She didn't push it like that again. I had to put her on my timeline a few times and remind her what the consequences were if she didn't behave. Essentially, I was setting her up to fail so that she'd learn on my schedule. And she did.

If you give your kids limits and let them know they'll be held accountable, it's absolutely amazing how self-possessed they become. They want to feel like they have a choice, that they have agency. Give it to them, respect them as people with free will, and you'll be amazed at what they can do.

I see it in GiGi every day. Someone gave her a chance and an opportunity to prove herself, and she grabbed it and didn't look back. She wouldn't and couldn't be where she is now, as she is now, if it had happened any other way. You can do this for your children too. As parents, we want to protect and coddle and do everything for our kids; it's second nature. But the only way for them to truly grow is for us to let go and encourage them to each be their own person. We have to stop peeling their grapes and skinning their hot dogs, and trust them to take care of themselves!

At the GiGi's National Conference this November, Paul and I sat at a table, listening to people speak, and I looked over at GiGi. She was sitting in a sequined halter dress she'd picked out, with her hair all done up in a side ponytail, and her legs crossed. She was the very picture of poise. I nudged Paul. "Look at her," I said. "Who is this girl? How did she get to this point?"

Paul smiled. "She did it herself," he said.

I realized he was right. GiGi is who she is because we let her be. We didn't put any limits on her, and look at what an amazing young woman she's become.

This is what Generation G is all about. All the things I see for the future, and all the work that has yet to be done will come about because of Generation G. We like to say that Generation G is a movement, a mind-set, and an action plan. And it really is all three. Ideas are great, but if you don't have a plan for how to implement them, you're not going to get anywhere. The motto of Generation G is "Changing the world one child, one diagnosis, one community at a time."

In our quest for global acceptance for all, we've launched this initiative that stands for people of all abilities, and their rights to dignity, opportunity, and global acceptance. We want to work to find the inner strength to harness the good in people and take action. And, finally, we want to engage families, volunteers, donors, millennials, visionary corporations, schools, the media, and anyone else to reshape perception and foster generosity for future generations to come. Generation G is about taking action. It's about committing to help, in whatever way you can, to make the world a place of global acceptance for all.

Way back in the beginning of this book I said that I believed that people genuinely wanted to do good, but it wasn't always easy for them to find the right thing to do. Generation G is about helping them discover ways they can help make the world a better place. It doesn't have to be about Down syndrome. Take your kids to visit a nursing home, volunteer at a soup kitchen, collect blankets for a homeless shelter, help someone struggling with homework—the opportunities are endless!

I see the amazing change in people every time they set foot in a GiGi's Playhouse. People walk out transformed. Suddenly, they have an understanding of what our kids are going through, and they understand why it's working. That's why so many of our college-age volunteers change their majors and become advocates for our kids. They understand what's happening. They see these amazing kids, and they don't want them to be made fun of. We're creating legions of people who will be like a group of middle-school basketball players in Kenosha, Wisconsin. These young teens confronted members of the crowd who were heckling a fourteen-year-old cheerleader with Down syndrome. The Playhouse allows people to see the beauty and potential of our kids. It makes you want to protect and empower them when you see what they can do. That's Generation G. It's about supporting each other, being kind, generous, and accepting.

Again, I have always gotten my inspiration from GiGi herself. And she is the perfect example of someone who is truly part of Generation G. Kindhearted, loving, and warm, GiGi is also one of the most generous people I know. Who knows if I'd even be here doing what I'm doing if I didn't see her give to others every day! If I didn't learn from her example, who's to say if GiGi's Playhouse would even exist? GiGi shows me how we can all be better. We can all lead by example. Show your kids what it's like to be a part of Generation G. Show them how to empower someone else or how to give back. Before you know it, your whole family will be part of Generation G!

That is my ultimate hope. If you get nothing else from this book, I hope that you will at least make a pledge right now to help those in need, and to befriend and defend those who need you. Do it with your kids. Do it with your family. Draw a letter *G* on your hand and enclose it in a heart. Take a picture and post it to social media with the hashtag #GenerationG. That's all it takes. Talk with your kids about what kind of a family you want to be. Talk about what you want to be remembered for. What do you want your legacy to be? There is something that literally everyone can do to work toward greater global acceptance for all. You can do it too. Join us as part of Generation G. If all of us work together, we can continue to change the world!

It starts with a pledge to be part of Generation G. That is the future. I still believe it's bright and boundless—but that will only prove true if we work together to make it so.

C H A P T E R   1 2

Looking Ahead—The Bright and Boundless Future

Generation G is the first step toward the future. It's a big, important step; one that is actually a step and a path at the same time, if that makes sense. At the end of the path? Who knows? The future is always an unknown, but I feel confident the future for GiGi's—and Generation G—is bright and boundless. I can't deny that I have big dreams for GiGi's. I'd love for there to be a GiGi's Playhouse presence in every metro market around the country. It certainly seems possible. We're expanding at such a rapid rate—in 2018 we have more than forty locations in the United States—that it's within our grasp to put a GiGi's Playhouse in every city in America. We could help so many people! Beyond that, what I really want is a way to serve those families and children who don't live in cities. While roughly 80 percent of Americans live in urban areas, that still leaves 20 percent of the population without access to city infrastructure, services, and community support. I want to help those people as well. I'd love to have some kind of mobile programming, a GiGi's bus, or fleet of buses, that drive around the rural areas of the country to provide therapy and programming to those kids and families who need it. Wouldn't that be amazing? I think about the people we could be reaching if we were able to go to them, instead of having them come to us, and I am overwhelmed by the possibility.

Years ago, it might have seemed like a crazy dream, but it's now a real possibility. Companies set up mobile medical clinics to drive around and conduct blood drives and provide mammograms. Is this so different? Meeting people where they are and meeting their needs: that's all we're trying to do! We already have three fifty-five-foot GiGi's trucks and a Jeep driving around and raising awareness of GiGi's Playhouse and Down syndrome achievement. Why can't we get a few more vehicles, and bring our therapists and programs to the people?

I would love to expand our international program as well. I want to bridge oceans, create connections, and change the world! You already know that, of course! As of now, our one international location is in Mexico. The Queretaro Playhouse is doing great, but people have to take buses for three or four hours to get there. We need to do more. We need to be in more places, in more countries, in more communities. We need a team behind the effort. Personally, I know nothing about international laws and taxes, and if we're going to expand globally, we need to bring someone on board who understands the intricacies of working in other countries. Children all over the world will benefit from the launch of more international locations, but we have to be smart about it. We have to make sure that we're meeting the needs of the international community and the families who live there.

For the time being, we can teach these purposeful, practical therapeutic applications to the kids at our Playhouses, and then they can bring what they learn home with them. I want what we teach and provide to be available to everyone, on our website, regardless of any individual situation. We don't charge people for any of our programming at the Playhouse, so why can't we put what we're doing online so that anyone can use it free of charge? And I'm not just talking about the Down syndrome community; I'm talking about everyone. A greater, more useful web presence can be so helpful to so many people.

It's not that hard! Remember the balance line I mentioned? That's a great example. Suddenly, it's not something that's helping your child at the Playhouse for a few hours a week. It can be something he or she does every day—several times a day. It's going to make a big difference and not take time out of any parent's day.

As I've already shown, once these kinds of therapies are brought into the home and made into practical, purposeful applications that become a part of the daily routine, the change will be dramatic. Time and time again, we've seen that the best way to learn something is through repetition. Once you train your body to do something, it becomes natural. We're well on our way to making that happen with our methods of practical, home-based therapy, but we still have a long way to go. I compare this sort of home-based therapy to how diabetics learn to manage their insulin levels at home. They don't need to go to the doctor every time they need to check their blood sugar levels; they can do all of it at home, with home-based therapy. We can do the same thing. We can build this into everyday life. It will not replace all the therapy that's needed, but it will be that little extra that can help our kids be all that they can be.

I'd also love to see a branded clothing line for our kids, specifically athletic clothes. This might seem unnecessary, but our kids do not fit into typical clothes. With their low muscle tone and shorter arms and legs, athletic clothes made for typical children don't fit our kids properly. This is just another example of our kids not quite fitting into this world, and the world not meeting them, even halfway. But it's a simple fix. What if Nike or Adidas or Under Armour wanted to work with us to develop a line of athletic clothing specifically for people with Down syndrome, or anyone with a similar build? This is where

I need to start dreaming big, because this is something we can't do on our own. We need buy-in from corporate America. We need a big corporation to see the value in what we're doing and decide to be a part of it. We need a big company to lead the way in becoming part of Generation G.

It'd be great for corporations as well! People with special needs make up the world's largest minority population, and virtually no one is creating things for them. It's a completely untapped market. What if we worked with Nike to launch G-Fit or G-Power! I can see it now: our kids modeling athletic clothes made just for them.

Our kids want to wear what their friends are wearing. They want to dress like their sisters and brothers. If they feel confident in how they look, there's no telling what they can do! You know what I'm talking about. We all have our favorite pair of jeans or a sweater that we love, and when we wear it, we feel great. The same is true for athletic clothes. When you're dressed in clothes that fit well and are designed to help you get the best workout possible, you're more likely to work hard. Our kids are the same way. The way you dress sets the tone for your entire day. The same thing happens to our kids. When they're dressed in something that makes them feel good—and fits them properly—it makes a huge difference. I've seen it in GiGi and our other kids. It really does make a difference.

All of this is about making things easier for parents to help their kids. If we can remove some of the built-in distractions that are inherent in raising a child with Down syndrome, it's that much easier for parents to give their children the tools they need to be successful. Make clothes that fit, give them a way to practice balance at home, take a few more decisions or steps off a parent's to-do list, and it all becomes more manageable.

I've already shared what it felt like to be a scared mother wishing that there was someone I could talk to who would make sure I had everything I needed, or a place I could go where those needs would be met. I've never forgotten that feeling. I feel it again every time a new mother comes into a Playhouse. I want to make her job easier so that she can focus on enjoying and empowering her child.

People genuinely want to help. I believe that, and I think many people are part of Generation G without even knowing it. It's a feeling and a desire we have in our hearts, an intention to make things better.

Sometimes I feel this desire in unexpected places. A few months ago, I was shopping in Target, and I saw a young boy with his grandmother. I noticed his walking stick and realized that he was blind. I thought to myself, *You don't see that very much. Why is that? I'm sure there are a lot of Children who are blind, but we never see them. Where are they all?* I'm immersed in the world of Down syndrome, so, naturally, I see it everywhere, but I couldn't remember the last time I'd seen a child who is blind. I wondered if the world accepted him, or if he struggled like GiGi. While he couldn't see other people reacting to what made him different, the people who love him certainly saw it. I knew exactly what that felt like.

I watched the boy as he walked along, smiling and holding his grandmother's hand. They passed the cooler where someone had just opened the door, and he must have felt the rush of cold air. He stopped and said, "Grandma, what was that?" I stopped dead in my tracks and watched the boy interact with his grandmother. She said lovingly, "Someone just opened the freezer door, honey." Watching the boy smile and walk away with his grandmother, I thought, *I hope this boy and his family have everything they need.*

This was not so different than what we've fought for at GiGi's. We want people to have access to the help and resources they need. Ultimately, that is the legacy of GiGi's Playhouse. I know that if I can do this, other parents can do it too. If we can help them get into the communities we're in, and if we can provide a place to celebrate achievements, that's what we're going to do. GiGi's exists to serve and help others.

This whole process can be incredibly overwhelming, but that's why we've started Generation G. If being kind, generous, and accepting makes it even a tiny bit better for someone else, this is all worth it. I want people to follow the path we blazed; I don't want them to have to start from scratch. We don't need to reinvent the wheel; we need to help each other. I never want anyone to think, *I'm not strong enough;*

or, *There aren't any people out there who will help me.* None of that is true. We are each strong, and there will *always* be someone who will help. Generation G is here for everyone—including you!

Recently, I was reminded, in quite a sobering way, of how far we have yet to go. At our national conference in Chicago this past November, our marketing manager gave a presentation that underscored very clearly how much road is still ahead of us. In a search engine on his laptop, he typed "bullying and Down syndrome." In less than a second, more than 785,000 articles appeared. Everyone was shocked. I take heart in the fact that some of these articles were about situations in which people stood up against bullies and defended people with Down syndrome. One article was about the middle-school basketball players in Kenosha, Wisconsin, that I mentioned earlier—the ones who confronted members of the crowd heckling a fourteen-year-old cheerleader with Down syndrome. These are the kinds of stories we need more of. In fact, we honored this entire team and school officials at our National Gala, and gave the entire team a Hero Award. There was not a dry eye in the house, and these young boys' lives were forever changed. They had a choice, and they chose to defend that girl. We are so grateful they did. Little by little, we're making progress, but we're not yet where we ultimately want to be.

I think that a lot of the hurtful language is unintentional. In another demonstration, Mark searched for the word *retard* on Twitter. He left his computer open, and, within two hours, the word had been used more than seven hundred times. Many of the tweets were from people joking around with their friends or calling them names. People don't think about the origins of the word or how hurtful it can be. We all need to be better. And it starts with acceptance and education. It starts with a pledge to be part of Generation G. That *is* the future. I still believe it's bright and boundless—but that will only prove true if we work together to make it so.

Conclusion

Even though my title has letters in it now, and I'm in charge of this multimillion-dollar international nonprofit organization, I still introduce myself as GiGi's mom because, at the end of the day, that is my most important job.

I realize that everything that has happened in my life—each success, failure, and diagnosis—brought me to where I am today. When you're in the middle of something, it's easy to think that you'll never get through it, but if I have learned anything, it's that you *will* get through it. Even more important than that, when you get through something, you grow and you learn and you become a stronger and better person because of it. Everything in my life has happened so that I could prepare for this, so that I could help and serve.

Some people read scripture and use those words to inspire themselves and others. Not that scripture hasn't helped me at times, but sometimes I like my scripture disguised in a country song and a bottle of wine. Rodney Atkins has a song that's always helped me. In it, he sings, "If you're goin' through hell, keep on going. Don't slow down if you're scared, don't show it." That's always helped me to push through, move forward, and keep on going.

The most important thing my mother ever taught us was the Golden Rule: "Do unto others as you would have them do unto you." She drilled it into us at every possible opportunity. As a result, I have very high expectations for people, and I push myself just as hard. I expect a lot from everyone because I know that if people with Down syndrome can step up and work hard and push, push, push, the rest of us have absolutely no excuse for coasting. And what I've found is that our kids want so badly to achieve and to be held to a higher standard. They want nothing more than to prove that they can do it. Often, it's the typical people who don't want to be challenged. That's what we've got to work on because this only works if we *all* step up.

There are times when I feel as though I have developed intolerance toward the way the world treats our kids. I have to make a conscious effort not to be resentful of certain things. The fact is that it's very unlikely that we'll ever have a celebrity as the face of Down syndrome to bring awareness to the diagnosis because, with prenatal testing, there are so many fewer opportunities. So it's not going to be a famous person standing next to his or her child with Down syndrome who brings this topic to the forefront. Instead, it's going to be a generational change, Generation G. We have to depend on others—sisters and brothers and moms and dads and grandparents and friends—to bring about this change. There's no celebrity spokesperson. It's all of us, working together. This goes right back to what happened with Bella when she stood up to her classmate and took the opportunity to educate. She's part of an army of acceptance we're creating. Maybe, someday, a celebrity *will* want to join us and be part of this movement. We'd love to have a celebrity spokesperson, but all believers—famous or otherwise—are welcome.

There are moments when it's hard, of course—and then there are moments when I realize that it's all worth it. The other day, I took GiGi shopping because she had been talking about how she needed "popular clothes." She went straight to the career section at the store and fixated on this pink silk blouse, very polished, very professional. She told me, "This is for when I'm speaking somewhere. It's silk." And I realized she knows exactly what her role is. She knows her responsibility, and she embraces it wholeheartedly.

As I watched her leave for school this morning, I noticed that she'd paired the blouse with a jean jacket, dressing it down and making it appropriate for school. Before she walked out the door, I had to stop myself from asking her, "Do you have your phone? Your homework? Everything you need?" Because I knew she did. She always does. I watched her walk out the door and to the bus stop, and I felt so proud. Of course she has everything she needs! She's a strong, beautiful teenager in her popular clothes, and she is ready to take on the world. I can't wait to see what she does.

There have been times when I have doubted whether I had any business writing a book. Often, it felt very conceited or arrogant, and I questioned whether anyone would want to read this story. But then, this past week, everything was brought into focus for me. We opened two new GiGi's locations in one weekend, opened a GiGi University at another location, and saw the GiGi's Playhouse truck driving across the country and spreading our message of universal acceptance for all. And at each of these locations, I saw the faces of the people who have been working so hard for all that we've accomplished. They keep thanking me, when all I want to do is thank them—they are the ones who are building Playhouses in their communities; they have made everything come together. So much of this feels like it's happening inside my little circle, with me spinning around like a crazy person and trying to keep it all together, but the fact is that it is being replicated over and over. If people knew how much love everyone else pours into this, they would understand that there's no limit to what we could do. It's the love and support and community effort that makes it all possible. And that, finally, is what convinced me that this story needed to be told. Because as much as it's my story and GiGi's story, it's the story of so many other people who care and love and sweat and cry and give, every single day. I want to honor them. I want them to share the limelight. They've earned this. They are the leaders of Generation G, and they are going to do amazing things.

And if you're reading this book, that means you're a part of Generation G too. You care, and you want to make a difference. Let's do this together!

CPSIA information can be obtained
at www.ICGtesting.com
Printed in the USA
LVOW03*1821140318
569871LV00005B/6/P